As an Angel of Light

Brian McCallum

Unless otherwise indicated, all scripture quotations are taken from the *King James Version* of the Bible. Public domain.

27 26 25 24 23 22 21   08 07 06 05 04 03 02

As an Angel of Light
ISBN-13: 978-0-89276-937-7
ISBN-10: 0-89276-937-8

Copyright © 2000, 2018 Rhema Bible Church
AKA Kenneth Hagin Ministries, Inc.
First edition 2000. Second edition 2018
Printed in the USA

In the U.S. write:
Kenneth Hagin Ministries
P.O. Box 50126
Tulsa, OK 74150-0126
1-888-28-FAITH
rhema.org

In Canada write:
Kenneth Hagin Ministries of Canada
P.O. Box 335, Station D
Etobicoke (Toronto), Ontario
Canada M9A 4X3
1-866-70-RHEMA
rhemacanada.org

Contents

Foreword

" *F*aith cometh by hearing, and hearing by the word of God," according to Romans 10:17.

Notice the phrase *"hearing and hearing."* These verbs are action words, and they are in the present tense. Especially notice that the verb "hearing" is repeated, indicating the necessity for repeating the action.

In this book, I have endeavored to acquaint readers with the importance of knowing their position in Christ—authority—a position that was given by our Father God and our Lord Jesus Christ.

Second, I have sought to acquaint readers with the need to fight the good fight of faith against the devices of Satan, our adversary—and a diligent enemy he is.

Third, I have opened the scriptures with the help of the Holy Spirit concerning the many devices the devil uses against our lives and ministries. Most of these devices are studied and illustrated here for readers' strengthening, edification, and knowledge.

As disciples of Jesus Christ, we cannot afford to be ignorant or careless concerning Satan's present position, activities (devices), or character.

While reading this book, you will find many exhortations to continue in faith or in God's Word. It is no mistake that this is emphasized so much; the Bible does so repeatedly. Remember, faith comes by hearing (present tense) and hearing and hearing, *ad infinitum.*

Brian K. McCallum

Brian K. McCallum

1

Sources of Power In the Universe

We are going to look at the known sources of power in the universe to learn who is really powerful.

God is the ultimate source of power and authority in the universe. All power comes from Him. Much power today is misused, but that doesn't mean it didn't originate with God. Nothing in the universe would be powerful if God had not made it to be powerful.

Is there anyone else who is all-powerful? What about the devil —is he all-powerful? No, he isn't, although you would think he is, the way some people act. You would think they don't know that in Christ they are strong in God's might.

You are not powerful in your natural self. You are no match for the devil in the natural realm. Your understanding in the natural realm is not equal to deal with him.

That's not where you have power. Power in your life comes from the fact that you are dwelling, walking, living, moving, and having your being in Christ. As you walk in the Spirit, power and authority are present in your life. It takes both of these things to get the job done.

God is the ultimate source of power and authority in the universe. His Word grants authority and tells us where power is resident.

We see in Revelation 19:6 that God is omnipotent: *"I heard as it were the voice of a great multitude, and as the voice of many waters, and as the voice of mighty thunderings, saying, Alleluia: for the Lord God omnipotent reigneth."*

All the created beings in Heaven are praising God, and they are calling Him *"the Lord God omnipotent."* At this point in Revelation,

God has brought all things to perfection in the saints. Jesus is beginning to reign on earth as King of kings. The government is fully in His hands. His omnipotence has manifested all of these works.

God's Unlimited Power

So God is the omnipotent One. "Omnipotent" means all-powerful — *all*-powerful. There is no limit to the power of God. We cannot grasp that truth completely because our understanding is finite, and God is infinite.

A natural mind cannot grasp this. Even a renewed natural mind cannot fully grasp what "all power" really means, but God reveals it to us in His Word.

However, your spirit man can grasp this concept and rest in it. You are living in Christ, and in Him all power is resident. The Lord God omnipotent reigns in you and through you to do His will on earth. It is important to remember that.

When you are dealing with some of the residents of the kingdom of darkness, they can seem awesome in the natural. However, some of them are lesser beings that don't seem so awesome.

None of them can be dealt with successfully with human under-standing. All of them must be dealt with by the Word of God and from living, moving, and having your being in Christ, empowered by the Greater One Who resides within you.

The Battle's Won

Greater is He Who is in us than any other being. If God is on our side, we already know who wins, don't we?

When we are fighting and wrestling with powers and principali-ties, as the Word of God says, we are not engaged in a contest to see who wins.

We already know we are winners in Him. We already know Jesus has defeated the powers of darkness and made a show of them openly. We already know He delivered us from all the powers and the authority of darkness when He translated us into His kingdom.

When were you translated into His kingdom? When you were born again. From that day on, you had a place in Him far above all principality, power, might, and dominion.

You are not wrestling with the devil in the dust to see who is going to come out on top. It has already been determined. You command him; you don't persuade him. You don't persuade God, either. He's already persuaded.

Warfare in the Mind

Who, then, needs to be persuaded? Your mind is what needs to be persuaded. That's where the warfare is. It's not out in the heavenly places somewhere.

You are not going out in the heavenlies pulling down principalities, evil spirits, and things like that. Where would you put them if you did? *It's in the mind where warfare takes place.* It's in the mind where you fight the good fight of faith. We will see this as we look further in God's Word.

2 CORINTHIANS 10:3–5

3 For though we walk in the flesh, we do not war after the flesh:

4 (For the weapons of our warfare are not carnal, but mighty through God to the pulling down of strong holds;)

5 Casting down imaginations, and every high thing that exalteth itself against the knowledge of God, and bringing into captivity every thought to the obedience of Christ.

Always come back to this fact: You are living, moving, and having your being in Christ, and all power is resident in Him. Any other being is much less powerful than He. Any other being has a defined limit to its power. God has no limit, and it is His power that delivers you!

How God Uses His Power

In Genesis 1:1, you see how God uses His power. The first verse says, *"In the beginning God created."* We wouldn't have to read any further to see one way He uses His power: He creates. He is the Creator, the only Creator. There is no other.

You say, "I can live in His creative power." Yes, you can. You can speak what the Word says, and God will perform His Word for you. But that doesn't make *you* the Creator. Many people have gotten off track about that over the years.

The devil got off track about it in the beginning, and now he is trying to draw people off track about the same thing. You don't become the Creator because you believe and speak God's words and He performs them.

God is the Creator, the only Creator. He is God alone, the Word of God says. No one will ever take His place. When the devil was the highest of all the created angelic beings, he thought he was going to take God's place. He didn't begin with this thought, but he got to the place where he thought he could remove God from His throne and take over Heaven.

Did Lucifer overthrow God's kingdom? No! There is no being that can do it. God is God alone. He is omnipotent. He is the Creator. Throughout scripture, we find that He uses that power creatively. You are blessed to have a part in it, but you must understand that it is His power that does the work.

Jesus Shows Us the Father

As Jesus walked this earth, what did He show us? He showed us the Father. Remember what Philip said to Jesus one day? "Lord, show us the Father, and that will be enough for us. If you will just show us the Father, we will understand."

Jesus replied, *"Have I been so long time with you, and yet hast thou not known me, Philip? He that hath seen me hath seen the Father"* (John 14:9).

If you see Jesus Christ walking this earth, you see the Father God in character and an exact performance of what God is, without any deviation. You also see the power of God resting upon Jesus to do the works.

Acts 10:38 says, *"How God anointed Jesus of Nazareth with the Holy Ghost and with power."* There's that word "power" again. God anointed Jesus with power. What are you anointed with? Power!

Turning to Acts 1:8, we read that Jesus told His disciples, *"But ye shall receive power, after that the Holy Ghost is come upon you: and ye shall be witnesses."* Whose power? God's power. Where? Upon you. The power is given for you to become a witness.

Overcoming Power

You need power to serve God in ministry and to serve Him through your personal growth. Without that power, you will not grow up unto the measure of the fullness of the stature of Christ. But with that power, you will.

It's an overcoming power. It overcomes all the indulgences and the limitations of the flesh as well as activity of other spirits. You need that power operating in your life. Jesus said, "You will be a witness when you have that power upon you." You will be a witness of God, not a witness of man.

ACTS 1:8

8 But ye shall receive power, after that the Holy Ghost is come upon you: and ye shall be witnesses unto me both in Jerusalem, and in all Judaea, and in Samaria, and unto the uttermost part of the earth.

Witnessing isn't the only thing you will do with God's power, although it is part of it. That power, Jesus said, will come upon you when the Holy Ghost comes upon you.

Acts 10:38 describes what happened when the Holy Ghost came upon Jesus: *"How God anointed Jesus of Nazareth with the Holy Ghost and with power: who went about doing good, and healing all that were oppressed of the devil; for God was with him."*

Submitting to God's Will

Did Jesus do anything He felt like? No, the Word says He did *good.* And as we read in Hebrews 10:9, He always did the will of the Father. He said, *"Lo, I come to do thy will, O God."*

Jesus didn't come to do His own will, even though there was nothing wrong or sinful with His will. Nothing was lacking in His will. But He submitted His own will, being a human being who was endowed with a will of His own. He submitted that ability to make choices to His Father— always, always, always, even unto His death on the cross. Despising the shame, He endured the cross for us so He could do the will of the Father.

Your will needs to be just as submitted, not any less submitted, to God. It is not right to go around with 99 percent of your will submitted and 1 percent, or even one-tenth of 1 percent, not submitted.

Granted, you are in the process of learning what submission is and how to submit. But when you know what the will of God is, and you won't submit yourself to it, you're in rebellion against God. What God asks is that you be submitted to what you know. Since what you know is always increasing, it always requires your increased submission to God.

When the Devil Flees

James 4:7 says, *"Submit yourselves therefore to God. Resist the devil, and he will flee from you."* This only works if you are submitted to

God. The devil won't flee from someone who isn't submitted to God. He doesn't need to, because they're powerless, and he knows it. He knows who is powerful and who is powerless.

Some people talk a lot, but they haven't come to the place where they've really submitted their lives to God. And until they do, they won't find they have authority.

But when you are in submission to God and you speak the Word of God—*wow!* It comes to pass as far as the devil is concerned. You're not trying to persuade him to do something; you're commanding him to do it in Christ because of what Jesus did.

God anointed Jesus with the Holy Ghost and with power, and He went about doing good. That's what God does with His power: He does good. Everything you ever saw God do in the Bible is good.

When God Judges

"What about when God had to judge His own people—the children of Israel—was that evil?"

No, that was good. It was necessary. There was no other way for Him to correct them except by what He did.

Everything God has ever done with the power He has is good, and He will never do anything other than good with it. I'm glad God doesn't lose control of Himself. We'd all be obliterated if He did!

When we think of getting upset, we think of losing our temper. God has never lost His, and I'm certainly glad He hasn't, because I can think of a few times when I would have been zapped by a thunderbolt if He had.

God always does what His Word says. He feels wrath against sin. The Bible says He is long-suffering, but that doesn't mean He doesn't have a temper. Even so, He never loses control of Himself like bad-tempered human beings do. God has never lost control, and He never will.

Remember, Jesus went about doing good and healing all that were oppressed of the devil, for God was with Him.

Our Better Covenant

"God, who at sundry times and in diverse manners spake in time past unto the fathers by the prophets" (Heb. 1:1). God did speak, and the prophets believed it. God saw their faith in what He had said to them, and He counted it to them as right standing.

Verse 2 continues, "[God] *hath in these last days spoken unto us by his Son."* Elsewhere in Hebrews and other places in the New Testament, it says this is a *better* covenant, founded on *better* promises. Did you ever ask yourself why they are better?

Did God heal people in the Old Testament? Yes. Does He heal us today? Yes. Did He save people in the Old Testament? Yes. Does He save us today? Yes.

However, people under the Old Covenant didn't get born again. They didn't get regenerated by the Holy Spirit like we have been, because that could not happen until Jesus rose from the dead; until He was regenerated by the Holy Spirit. He is now the first begotten of many sons like Himself.

Why is ours a better covenant? Is it just because we're born again? That's one part of it, but everything that God had promised about Christ at His first coming has already been fulfilled. He defeated all the principalities and powers and made a show of them openly (Col. 2:15).

The fallen spirits that had been given authority by Adam's disobedience no longer have that authority. It was taken away from them, and we have received authority in the earth by the Word of God. God gave it to us because of Jesus.

God has spoken to us by His Son. Jesus came to dwell or "tabernacle" in us, not in a place made with man's hands. Under the New Covenant, we don't need to go to Jerusalem to worship. We worship within ourselves, because that is where God is living.

"Exceeding Great and Precious Promises"

Ours is a better covenant, because the promises have been fulfilled. They are really provisions made for us—"exceeding great and precious promises"—and they have been fulfilled to us in Christ (2 Peter 1:4). We simply believe and receive what God has said He has done.

Jewish people who lived before the time of the cross looked forward to the coming of their Messiah, but they never experienced the fullness of His coming; only a measure of it blessed them.

Thank God, they were blessed like they were, and thank God they believed as they did. But we can go beyond that, because He lives in us, and we are living in Him.

Our New Covenant is founded on the provisions Christ made for all who believe in Him. He is the heir of all things, according to Hebrews 1:2, and the Word of God says further in Romans 8:17 that we are heirs *and* joint-heirs with Him! This means you are a joint-heir with the risen Savior!

One of those who lived under the Old Covenant and looked forward to the coming of the Messiah was Job. Job boldly declared, *"I know that my redeemer liveth, and that he shall stand in the latter day upon the earth"* (Job 19:25).

Believing Jews knew that their Messiah would come. We can look back and know His first coming has already happened, and we can enjoy all the blessings of His first coming.

Upholding All Things

God, the Creator of the worlds, *"hath in these last days spoken unto us by his Son...by whom also he made the worlds; Who being the brightness of his glory, and the express image of his person, and upholding all things by the word of his power"* (Heb. 1:2–3).

Jesus Christ is God's Word. John 1:1 says, *"In the beginning was the Word, and the Word was with God, and the Word was God."* Jesus is the Word of God, and He upholds everything by the Word of His power.

Colossians 1:17 tells us, *"by him all things consist."* Rotherham's version of that verse says, *"by him all things are being held together."*

Did you know that if Jesus wasn't alive, the world wouldn't exist? It would fly apart! It wouldn't hold together any longer. It is all held together in Him, for He upholds all things by the Word of His power. Hebrews 1:3 concludes, *"when he had by himself purged our sins, [He] sat down on the right hand of the Majesty on high."*

Say What the Word Says

In the Book of Ephesians, we see more about God's power. You need to say what the Word says about you, and you need to say it out loud frequently. It's all right to meditate or "chew" on it in your mind, but don't neglect to say it out loud.

This is a passage of scripture I listen to myself say daily. It's from Ephesians 1:17–18:

EPHESIANS 1:17–18

17 That the God of our Lord Jesus Christ, the Father of glory, may give unto you the spirit of wisdom and revelation in the knowledge of him:

18 The eyes of your understanding being enlightened; that ye may know....

Knowing is what is important in this lifetime. We need to know certain things. We need to become fully persuaded and stay fully persuaded. If we continue in the Word, it will keep us fully persuaded.

The passage continues:

EPHESIANS 1:18–19

18 The eyes of your understanding being enlightened; that you may know what is the *hope of his calling*, and what the riches of the glory of his inheritance in the saints,

19 And what is the *exceeding greatness of his power* to usward who believe, according to the working of his mighty power.

There are three things listed here that God wants you to know. *First* is the hope of His calling. *Second* is the riches of the glory of His inheritance in the saints.

God's greatest inheritance is in the Church, the Body of Christ. He uses the Church to show His manifold, many-faceted wisdom to all the principalities and powers. He shows them how He brings the Church to perfection, making every part of His Body like Jesus.

Only One Outcome

Just like you know your own name in the natural, you need to know these things in the Spirit realm so you can command the inhabitants of darkness—evil spirits—not human beings.

You can command human beings in the Army, but you can't command people in the Body of Christ. (Not everyone obeys, even in the Army.) However, every resident of the kingdom of darkness must obey your command when you know the *third* point, which is the most important: the exceeding greatness of God's power.

You must be fully persuaded that when you speak the Word of God, there can be only one outcome. You won't have to command the devil 50 times. Once will be enough. Commanding him twice would be getting into unbelief. And the farther you go in that direction, the more unbelief you would be in.

You must know that when you command him, he must bow his knee to your command. You are doing it in the power Christ wrought for us.

That's what verses 19 and 20 tell us: Jesus wants you to *know* what is the exceeding greatness of His power. He doesn't want you to have simply heard about it.

Contacting God's Power

The first place you came in contact with God's power on your own was when you were regenerated or born again. What did God do? He made you a whole new creation!

Everything old—all the rotten things you ever did—passed away. In fact, everything you ever did passed away, because it was all rotten. I'm serious. Even the seemingly good things you did were done for the wrong reason.

When you were born again, you became a new creation. Old things disappeared. They're gone. They're in the sea of God's forgetfulness. God will never again touch them with His thought-life, and you shouldn't, either.

They are as far removed as the East is from the West. How far is that? Head East, and tell me when you get to the West. You'll keep going around and around, and you'll never get there. That's how far God has removed your sins from the you. Your whole past life was remitted or forgiven, the Bible teaches.

Of course, that doesn't mean you can't sin after being born again, but those sins, too, can be removed as far as the East is from the West if you repent and confess them to God.

Changed by the Power of God

How much did you know about God when you were born again? Probably very little; just enough to get born again. But look at what the power of God did when you responded to Him in faith: It changed you completely.

It made you a whole new creation in Christ, and the Holy Spirit began the process of completely changing your mind and soul, which will someday be fully completed even in the natural man.

When you think about it, you will realize you started out with God in an *instant*. When you believed, you were instantaneously regenerated. However, it will take a lifetime to get your soul brought completely in line with the Word of God, or renewed, as the Bible calls it. Then, in an instant, in the twinkling of an eye, your body will be changed at the resurrection or rapture of the Church.

So this process of regeneration starts in an instant, when you are born again, takes a lifetime, and then ends in an instant when Jesus returns and your spirit and body are reunited. Sometimes I think we'd like it if it happened in three instants!

However, that isn't the way God has ordained it, because He is perfecting something in your soul over a period of a lifetime. It takes that long to perfect, and it isn't perfect in an instant, as we'd like it to be. It isn't even perfect in 10 years. It's perfect in one lifetime.

When you finish your life, you will be perfected in the realm of the soul and fully grown spiritually. There aren't any shortcuts. However, the power of God is working in you during that entire period of time to transform you and renew your mind and soul, which are an important part of your eternal self.

Greek Words for "Power"

God wants you to know the exceeding greatness of His power. We are going to look at four words for "power" in the Greek language. The first is *dunamis*. We get the English word "dynamite" from it.

If you've got some dynamite, you treat it carefully, don't you? You don't carry it around in your back pocket. Neither do you place it on a hot stove when you're not using it! When you store it, you store it so far away from everything else that if it ignites, it won't damage anything.

That's the kind of idea this word *dunamis* conveys. It has the potential to show power at any instant—and that potential is in you! There is a potential manifestation of power in you at any instant if you know the exceeding greatness of His power.

His power doesn't have to be in manifestation 24 hours a day for you to know it; you know it because you know what the Word of God says. You know it because you know what God promised you. You know it because you have seen it manifested in other ways. You know its potential is there any time—any day you need it—as long as you are continuing in the Word of God.

I can't emphasize how important it is that you continue hearing the Word of God. Faith doesn't come by *having heard*; it comes by *hearing*, present tense.

Manifestations of Power in Your Life

God wants you to know the exceeding greatness of His power to those who believe, according to "the working." The word "working" in the Greek is *energia*. We get the English word "energy" from it. It means a performance, a manifestation of power, or a display.

There should be manifestations of power in your life every day, because you must overcome something every day. For example, you must overcome the tendencies of your flesh, keeping your body under and bringing it into subjection.

You must also overcome any satanic activity that arises—and you must overcome a world system whose agenda isn't in agreement with your Christian beliefs.

If you have favor in the world system, it is God Who gave it to you, not men, unless they are touched by God. If your ways are pleasing to God, and if you are walking in faith, He will affect men in such a way to give you favor. However, men in the world won't give favor to you out of the goodness of their hearts, because they don't have any goodness in their hearts.

God can even give you peace with your enemies, the Bible says. Unsaved people are potential enemies of yours, although you shouldn't fight them or treat them like enemies. I am merely pointing out that if they are not regenerated in their inward man, they are enemies of God in their hearts, and thus they are potential enemies of yours.

A Force at Work

So this word *energia* shows a display of power. There is a display of it daily in our lives, "according to the working of his *mighty* power."

The word "mighty" is the Greek word *iskus*, which means a force at work.

If I were to lean forward a little on a podium while teaching, there would be a force on that podium, even though it wouldn't be apparent. Then, if I leaned more forcefully on it, the podium would move. The force was already at work on it. If it hadn't been, the added force wouldn't have moved it.

Often that's the way it is in your life when you are dealing with something that needs to be changed. You've released faith from your heart, and you've spoken the Word of God. The force of faith went to

work immediately, whether you saw it or not, but it won't necessarily
accomplish what it was sent to do in an instant. We've all learned that
at one time or another.

That's what *iskus* conveys to us: The minute you speak the Word of
God, you have put a spiritual force to work. It will stay at work as long
as you continue in the Word, and it will accomplish what you have sent
it to do. Continuing in the Word gets the job done.

The Bible says that God watches over His Word to perform it; to see
that it comes to pass. Really, God is responsible for making it happen;
you are responsible for believing it and continuing to believe it. You
can't bring it to pass yourself.

Brother Kenneth E. Hagin is fond of saying, "There's nothing in my
own self that could even heal a gnat's wing, but God in me heals all the
time." It is God who performs His Word. He watches over it.

God's Power Is Unlimited

The fourth Greek word which has to do with different facets of
God's power and authority is *kratos*, the word translated "power."
This brings us back to where we started. The word we started with in
the Book of Revelation was "omnipotent." The omnipotence of God
is the power we are discussing. God will see to it that His Word comes
to pass, for He is all-powerful.

Nothing can deter God except unbelief on our part. We can limit
God by living in disobedience and unbelief, but when we live in faith,
there is no limit.

God will perform His Word, and everything He is will see to it
that His Word comes to pass. It's His responsibility to see to it that it
comes to pass when you're in faith about it.

This last word for "power," *kratos*, means ruling power, the power
of God which is far above all principality and power and might and

dominion and every name that is named, not only in this world, but also in that which is to come.

EPHESIANS 1:19
19 And what is the exceeding greatness of his power to usward who believe, according to the *working of his mighty power.*

2

How the Devil Uses His Power Today

We are now going to give the devil his "due." However, all that is "due" to him is perdition, as we see in the Word of God.

We have seen that God is omnipotent. Where are we living? In Him, so we know who is going to win any confrontation with evil before we go any further.

Nevertheless, we need to know the enemy, how he became what he is, what he is up to now, and what his devices are to try to draw us away from God. Paul wrote, *"we are not ignorant of his devices"* (2 Cor. 2:11).

Some people ask, "Why do you study the devil so much?" We don't study him that much. Knowing about him is simply one part of the counsel of God found in the Word. We do not concentrate on the devil. We do not try to make people devil-conscious, looking for a demon behind every bush or in everything that happens.

Actually, the devil doesn't necessarily cause everything bad that happens. Human beings themselves cause many bad things. The fact that the world is under a curse is another reason why bad things happen.

But you do need to recognize the devil's activity. You need to recognize him when he is present; you need to know how to deal with him scripturally; and you need to know what your place is in relation to his activity.

Limited Authority

First of all, the devil has limited authority. He is not all-powerful; nevertheless, he must be considered a powerful being, because he

is a spirit being. If you don't deal with him by the Holy Spirit—if
you don't walk in and by the power of the Spirit—you will not be
successful.

In other words, if you walk in the flesh and try to deal with the
devil, telling him to go to hell all the time, that's just your flesh talking.
It won't accomplish anything in dealing with the devil.

You won't be able to deal with the devil with your own understanding in the natural realm. You must move in the Spirit realm to deal with
him—and you must know who you are in Christ. You must stay in contact with God, with your eyes on Jesus, when you deal with the devil.

Hebrews 12:1 speaks of running your race. When you do, always
run your race with your eyes on Jesus. No matter how you are dealing
with principalities, powers, rulers of darkness of this world, and so
forth, don't get sidetracked. Don't take your attention away from the
Word of God when you are dealing with the devil. Don't amplify the
problem; amplify the solution.

Don't Give Place to the Devil

According to the Word of God, the devil has authority to move in
the kingdom of darkness only as people give him place to operate.

Ephesians 4:27 warns, *"Neither give place to the devil."* To whom
was that written? To believers. It was not written to the world, because
the world gives place to the devil all the time—and they don't even
know they're doing it!

Before I was saved, I didn't believe there *was* a devil. He had me
wrapped up in darkness. Although I was giving him all kinds of place
to operate in my life, I didn't believe he existed!

I thought the devil was the figment of someone's imagination—a
creature with horns and a tail who wore a red suit and carried a
pitchfork.

As soon as you are saved, you find there really *is* a devil, and he is no figment of anyone's imagination. The devil is real; he is a spirit being; and he must be dealt with by your walking in the Spirit, believing and acting on the Word of God.

How Jesus Dealt With the Devil

How did Jesus deal with him? He constantly said, "Satan, it is written." When Jesus commanded devils to come out of people, they came out quickly, without any further conversation. The Bible says they sometimes "tore" the person before they left him—but they always obeyed what Jesus said.

When the wind and the waves roared and threatened to capsize the boat containing the disciples and Jesus, He remained asleep. That's how worried He was about it.

When the disciples woke Him up and said, *"Master, carest thou not that we perish?"* (Mark 4:38), He simply stood up and said, "Peace, be still."

He didn't hold a 24-hour prayer meeting to get His disciples to agree with Him. In the first place, they couldn't. Jesus knew better than to try to get them to agree with Him. He simply spoke the word of God to that situation, and it changed immediately.

He didn't have to fast and pray for two days to get ready to take his authority, because He was always ready. He *stayed* ready. And that's what you need to do: Stay ready!

Fasting and Praying

Of course, fasting and praying will help you stay ready and spiritually keen—and you should fast and pray—but some people get the idea you have to fast and pray to get devils to leave.

There are no devils you have to fast and pray to deal with. You do need to fast and pray to keep yourself ready to deal with anything.

When you command the devil or any of his cohorts with authority from your heart, they must obey.

The whole point of fasting and praying is that you then act from your heart, not from your head. A lot of people speak out of their heads, and then they worry because nothing happens. Nothing is going to happen when you speak out of your head. Faith doesn't come by having heard. Faith comes by hearing—continually hearing—the Word of God.

I can't emphasize enough how important it is for you to continue in the Word of God in every area of your life. You are to *live* by faith; you are not to use it only in emergencies.

You should be learning to submit yourself to that faith principle in every area of your life. Every breath you take, you take by faith.

You are not living by natural human life anymore; you have something better than that to live by. The life that you now live in the flesh you live by the faith of the Son of God. He lives in you. The faith principle works even in your natural body, and you need it.

There will be times when you will find that the natural human life isn't enough. You must tap into that place in God where you can overcome circumstances and negative events in the natural realm.

How the Devil Uses His Power

I want you to know how the devil uses his power today. We saw how God uses His power to do good, to create, and to bless. What do you think the devil does with the power he has? He comes to steal, kill, and destroy (John 10:10). When you see something going on, you know immediately who is behind it.

In the first chapter of Job, we see what the devil does when he has authority in a person's life. People give him authority themselves. That's why Paul said, *"Neither give place to the devil."*

Job gave the devil a place to operate in his life. Although the Word has been amplified to us—greater revelation is given to us today—the Word of God does not change. God's Word is the same yesterday, today, and forever (Heb. 13:8).

The devil wasn't specially authorized by God to attack Job to see what would happen. Some people read that into the Book of Job, but that is not what happened. In chapter 3, Job admitted that what he had greatly feared had come to pass.

Why Job was so afraid isn't explained, but the fact that he was afraid is definitely stated. He said in verses 25 and 26:

JOB 3:25–26
25 For the thing which I greatly feared is come upon me, and that which I was afraid of is come unto me.
26 I was not in safety, neither had I rest, neither was I quiet; yet trouble came.

Job's Learning Experience

If you are in great fear about something, you can't be in faith about it at the same time. Job was a blessed man. The Bible tells us so at the beginning of the Book of Job. Job was a a just man who believed God as far as his salvation went. However, like us, there were some things that Job needed to learn.

He learned these things in a period of about nine months, and they greatly blessed him the rest of his life. He lived a lot longer. At the time of his death, he was a very old man, almost 200 years old. He was blessed in the years following his testing, and everything he had lost was restored to him twofold.

Look what the devil did when he had access to Job. Job prayed earnestly for his children. Evidently, he was concerned about the way they lived. He continually prayed for them, because he was afraid they had sinned and cursed God in their hearts.

JOB 1:6–19

6 Now there was a day when the sons of God came to present themselves before the Lord, and Satan came also among them.

7 And the Lord said unto Satan, Whence comest thou? Then Satan answered the Lord, and said, From going to and fro in the earth, and from walking up and down in it.

8 And the Lord said unto Satan, Hast thou considered my servant Job, that there is none like him in the earth, a perfect and an upright man, one that feareth God, and escheweth [avoids] evil?

9 Then Satan answered the Lord, and said, Doth Job fear God for nought?

10 Hast not thou made an hedge about him, and about his house, and about all that he has on every side? thou hast blessed the work of his hands, and his substance is increased in the land.

11 But put forth thine hand now, and touch all that he hath, and he will curse thee to thy face.

12 And the Lord said unto Satan, Behold, all that he hath is in thy power; only upon himself put not forth thine hand. So Satan went forth from the presence of the Lord.

13 And there was a day when his sons and his daughters were eating and drinking wine in their eldest brother's house:

14 And there came a messenger unto Job, and said, The oxen were plowing, and the asses feeding beside them:

15 And the Sabeans [brutal raiders] fell upon them, and took them away; yea, they have slain the servants with the edge of the sword; and I only am escaped alone to tell thee.

16 While he was yet speaking, there came also another, and said, The fire of God is fallen from heaven [it wasn't the fire of God at all], and hath burned up the sheep, and the servants, and consumed them; and I only am escaped alone to tell thee.

17 While he was yet speaking, there came also another, and said, The Chaldeans made out three bands, and fell upon the camels, and have carried them away, yea, and slain the servants with the edge of the sword; and I only am escaped alone to tell thee.

18 While he was yet speaking, there came also another, and said, Thy sons and thy daughters were eating and drinking wine in their eldest brother's house:

19 And, behold, there came a great wind from the wilderness, and smote the four corners of the house, and it fell upon the young men, and they are dead; and I only am escaped alone to tell thee.

Acts of God?

Insurance companies always call disasters "acts of God." The tragedies that happened to Job weren't acts of God, yet that is what Job understood them to be. Job's understanding was not what ours is today. That's why we don't use Job's doctrine to live by: It won't work.

It worked for Job, because when he acted on what he knew, God could bless him; but we know much *more* than Job knew, and God expects us to act according to the knowledge we have today.

The things that happened to Job are a example of what the devil does with his power when he has access to a person's life. Again, he has come to steal, kill, and destroy. That's what he wants to do.

If the devil were all-powerful, as some people think, we would all be dead! If the devil could do *anything* he felt like, what chance would we have against him?

Fighting Fear

In Mark chapter 4, we see Satan attacking Jesus and His disciples with a great storm out in the middle of the Sea of Galilee. Verse 35 shows why you don't need to be afraid even if things don't look good: *"The same day, when the even was come, he saith unto them, Let us pass over unto the other side."*

If Jesus says, "Let's go across the lake to the other side," do you know where you're going? You're going to the other side! You're not going to go out in the middle of the lake and drown. You're going to reach the other side.

That's what I say when I get in an airplane, "I'm going over to the other side." I used to fly, and I never thought too much about the hazards, but now when I'm flying commercially with someone else in the cockpit, I think about it; especially when I read reports of some of the accidents pilots have been responsible for.

If you have faith, God will intervene on your behalf. *Faith is greater than natural things.* Faith affects and changes natural things.

MARK 4:35–38

35 He saith unto them, Let us pass over unto the other side.

36 And when they had sent away the multitude, they took him even as he was in the ship. And there were also with him other little ships.

37 And there arose a great storm of wind, and the waves beat into the ship, so that it was now full.

38 And he was in the hinder part of the ship, asleep on a pillow.

At the time the devil was doing his thing, stirring up winds and waves, Jesus was totally at peace.

When Destruction Comes

God established the rain cycle in the earth. He causes the wind to blow. We need the wind to blow so rain will come. We need the rain to water the ground so things will grow.

All of that is good, and that's why God put those things in the earth. However, God didn't establish the rain cycle here so we would have two feet of it in an hour. He didn't establish the weather cycle here so we would have tornadoes to blow our houses down.

That's the corruption of the rain or weather cycle, and it's caused by the enemy. He corrupts what is good, and he is responsible for the destruction that follows. God is not. God didn't establish weather patterns on earth to destroy mankind or his possessions. When destructive things happen, it's because God's creation has been corrupted.

The storm that arose on the Sea of Galilee was the work of the devil. Waves beat into the ship until it became full of water.

Jesus knew immediately what was happening when He awoke: *"He was in the hinder part of the ship, asleep on a pillow: and they awake him, and say unto him, Master, carest thou not that we perish? And he arose, and rebuked the wind"* (Mark 4:38–39). Jesus simply rebuked the wind. That rebuke came from His believing heart.

Conversing With Demons

"Peace, be still," Jesus said to the sea. Notice He spoke only three words. *You don't need to be wordy to deal with the devil.* Some people have the idea that to get people delivered from a devil, you've got to talk and yammer for hours. I know, because I used to be involved in this kind of deliverance ministry. If this error comes around again, just ignore it.

You don't need to talk to some devil for an hour to get him to come out of someone. He's going to lie to you anyway. How much better off are you going to be at the end of your conversation with him? All you're doing is focusing on what the devil is doing.

Instead, keep your focus where it belongs—on Jesus—and speak the Word of God with faith and confidence, like Jesus did, knowing that when you do, there can be only one result. That demon *must* bow his knee to the Word. He doesn't have any choice when the command comes from your heart.

As soon as Jesus spoke to the wind and the sea, what happened? The wind ceased, and the waves calmed down. Then Jesus addressed His disciples. *"And he said unto them, Why are ye so fearful? how is it that ye have no faith?"* (Mark 4:40). Sometimes Jesus said, "O ye of little faith, wherein did you doubt?" In other words, "You have some faith. Why didn't you use it?"

Fear vs. Faith

In this case, the disciples didn't have any faith. They were in fear. *When you're in fear, you don't have any faith.* Faith and fear cannot coexist. You can't be walking around in fear, acting in fear, and speaking in fear, and then say, "I'm in faith."

This doesn't mean you can't feel afraid and still be in faith. You can feel afraid and be in faith as long as you don't let how you *feel* determine what you *do* or *say.*

When you get around where the devil is operating, your skin will crawl. Your hair will stand straight up, if you have any. (I used to have enough to know that it did.)

This happens because your flesh is repulsed by his presence. It's not that your flesh is so good; it just doesn't like him. Did you know that none of his cohorts in his own kingdom like him? They all hate each other.

If you are in a place where the devil and other spirits are manifesting, your own flesh will tell you what is going on, but that doesn't mean you have to be afraid. You can have a sinking feeling in the pit of your stomach but still not be afraid.

If your heart is full of the Word of God, and if you have continued in the Word of God, what will happen when you feel that way? Out of your spirit will come strength, and that strength will sustain you, no matter how you feel.

A Manifestation of Evil

Feeling afraid is not *being* afraid. You can feel afraid and be in faith, but you cannot act or speak in fear and be in faith. Don't let how you feel determine what you do or say. If you're full of the Word, it won't.

I've had experiences along these lines. Once when I was running a school for troubled young people in California, I was called out to the school in the middle of the night. A youngster was sick, and I had to take him to the hospital.

All the regular employees had gone home or to sleep in their rooms, the students were in bed, and only the night watchman was up, watching over the place.

I left home, drove to the school, and picked up the young man to take him to the emergency room. My wife was the school nurse. I knew I was supposed to go into the health office and get the permission slip the boy's guardian or parents had signed to authorize health care if it was necessary. You can't get even minor health care in a lot of hospitals unless you have that form.

The boy was feeling so terrible, I forgot to get his form. I just took off for the hospital. But the doctors wouldn't treat him until I went back and got his permission slip. Fortunately, it was only a few miles back to the school.

When I got there, the night watchman told me, "You've got to come upstairs! Something really bad is going on up there." When I explained I had to rush back to the hospital, he offered to take the form to the hospital himself if I would go upstairs and straighten things out. I agreed, and up the stairs I went.

When I got to the top of the stairs, the hair on my head stood up. That's what the night watchman had sensed. It was clear that another spirit was in great manifestation.

The watchman had told me which room the disturbance was in. When I entered, the presence of evil was powerful. It was a large room containing three double bunks. In the corner ahead of me I saw a young man on the top bunk, as far back in the corner as he could get.

The three other occupants of the room were huddled together in the opposite corner, as far away from him as they could get. I could see they were scared out of their wits!

Exposed to Witchcraft

About a week before this, the 16-year-old boy in the first corner came to us from Modesto, California, where he had lived in a foster home—until his caseworker found out that he was living with a witch!

California licenses witches to be foster parents. (As you know, California leads the nation in all sorts of strange things.)

When the boy's caseworker found out he was in that situation, he brought him to us and enrolled him in our school. He was supposed to be with us for several months. His parents were dead, but his grandmother was living, and she was a Christian. She had prayed, and he had gotten saved even while living with the witch. That's why he was brought to us.

However, he had lived with the witch for about six months before any of this came to light. He had seen her call on a familiar spirit that worked through her and showed her where to find lost objects.

The boy had a ring his grandmother had given him, and it was very important to him. About a week before this manifestation happened, he came to me and told me that he had lost the ring. When things were missing, we looked through the belongings of the other young people in the room and searched the rest of the school. In this case, we didn't find the ring.

I called the boy to my office and said, "Here's what we'll do. We'll pray and ask the Lord to show us where the ring is. I know how important it is to you." I asked him, "Do you believe God will do that?" He replied, "Yes, I do. I believe He's a good God." So we prayed.

A few days later, the boy came to me and asked, "Has the Lord shown you anything?" I said, "No. Has He shown you anything?" "No, not yet."

I said, "Just wait. Don't be impatient. God will show you where the ring is, and He will see that it is returned to you."

Another two days went by, and he asked again. I still didn't know anything, and the boy was getting a little nervous, so he decided to take matters into his own hands.

Dealing With a Familiar Spirit

The night I was urged to investigate what was happening in his room, he'd called upon the familiar spirit he had seen the witch call upon, and it showed up! This is not something you should do. He learned that.

I simply spoke the Word of God over the situation, and the satanic manifestation stopped immediately. As fast as I said, "Depart from here in Jesus' Name," the demon activity stopped.

No matter how big, bad, or weird spirits are, they must obey the Word of God if you believe it when you speak it! They must bow their knee to the Name of Jesus. There are no two ways about it. You don't have to persuade them. You *command* them, as we have seen.

Although the demonic activity stopped, it took me until 3 a.m. to settle those guys down enough so they could go back to sleep. But the end of the story got better.

As soon as I got to my office later that morning, a knock came on the door. There stood one of the boy's three roommates. He said, "I've seen enough. How do you get saved?"

What the devil means for evil, God will use for good if someone will believe God in the midst of the situation. I led that young man to salvation in Jesus right then and there. And before that day was over, all three of the boy's roommates were saved!

However, it took me two weeks to restore the one who was already a Christian back into fellowship after he realized what he had done and how terrible it was. He just wouldn't forgive himself until he finally realized that grace is greater than all our sin.

The Devil's Devices

The Bible reports that some devils coming out of people tore them. The people foamed at the mouth, wallowed on the ground, and fell down like they were dead—but they were delivered. They weren't dead; they were delivered. Sometimes devils make a last attempt like that to try to hurt people, but they aren't successful.

In Mark chapter 4, we saw Satan himself try to attack the Lord and His disciples. He's not too smart, is he? In fact, the devil doesn't have any wisdom at all. Real wisdom comes from God. Satan has a lot of what the world considers worldly wisdom, but he is not wise. Why would you attack Jesus and think you were going to succeed?

Satan works through fallen angels—demons—and he works through men. Have you ever noticed that he works through human beings when he can get them to do his will?

Actually, man is a neutral power. He doesn't have power of his own, but he can tap into other sources of power—either the power of God or the power of the devil. He has the right and the authority to make such a choice. He has the potential to become part of the good or the evil. And you see people doing both every day.

Obeying From the Heart

Romans 6:16 is written to people who are becoming believers for the first time, but it also applies to people who are already believers:

ROMANS 6:16
16 Know ye not, that to whom ye yield yourselves servants to obey, his servants ye are to whom ye obey; whether of sin unto death, or of obedience unto righteousness?

You don't have to tell which is which. To obey the devil is to sin, and it will result in death. To obey God is a blessing, and it will result in His righteousness working through and in you.

The next verse says:

ROMANS 6:17
17 But God be thanked, that ye were the servants of sin, but ye have obeyed from the heart that form of doctrine which was delivered you.

What is "that form of doctrine"? We find the answer in Romans 10:8: *"But what saith it? The word is nigh thee, even in thy mouth, and in thy heart."*

In other words, the word that is in your mouth must come from your heart to do any good. It doesn't come from your head. It doesn't come from your having heard. No, you need to have fresh contact with God's Word all the time, like you do anything else. You need to continue in the Word.

The form of doctrine by which you receive or operate is always the same: *"That if thou shalt confess with thy mouth the Lord Jesus, and shalt believe in thine heart that God hath raised him from the dead, thou shalt be saved"* (Rom. 10:9).

The word "saved" means "delivered." The Greek word is *sosa,* and one of the meanings of that word is "to be delivered." Other meanings include "preserved, prospered in spirit, soul, and body, and kept unto God's eternal kingdom."

How To Receive From God

How is a person delivered? By believing in his heart and confessing with his mouth. That is how you partake of your inheritance of the saints in light (Col. 1:12). That is how you receive anything from God. And the way you minister in faith to others is also by believing in your heart and speaking what you believe with your mouth.

But the Word must be resident in your heart. That's why *continuing* in the Word is so important. You won't obey the form of doctrine from your heart unless the Word is resident there, so you need to continue in the Word and continually be full. Staying full of the Word is staying full of the Spirit.

Why? Because the words that Jesus speaks to us are not just words; they are *spirit and life.* Therefore, if you stay full of God's Word, you will be full of the Spirit, too.

ROMANS 10:10–11

10 For with the heart man believeth unto righteousness; and with the mouth confession is made unto salvation.

11 For the scripture saith, Whosoever believeth on him shall not be ashamed.

When you use that form of doctrine that has been delivered to you, and when you partake of your inheritance of the saints in light by speaking from your believing heart, you will never be sorry you did. You will always be glad you did. And you will never be ashamed that you stood in faith, depending on God at that moment, because He will perform His Word for you. He is watching over the Word you speak to perform it.

You don't have to perform it. Isn't that good news? I'm so glad to know I don't have to make it happen! Did you ever try to make the Word of God happen? If you tried, you know it doesn't work. God sees to it that it happens. All you need to do is keep in faith about it. Keeping in faith is continuing to speak over situations that need to be changed.

The Worst Choice

In Mark chapter 5, we find an example of how a man can make that choice. This is the most extreme biblical example I could think of to illustrate this. If you can see this man believing God and running to Jesus for deliverance, you can see anyone doing it.

MARK 5:1–4

1 And they came over unto the other side of the sea, into the country of the Gadarenes.

2 And when he was come out of the ship, immediately there met him out of the tombs a man with an unclean spirit,

3 Who had his dwelling among the tombs; and no man could bind him, no, not with chains:

4 Because that he had been often bound with fetters and chains, and the chains had been plucked asunder by him, and the fetters broken in pieces: neither could any man tame him.

Beyond Natural Strength

Imagine that! This man had often been bound with iron chains, but he would pop them apart with his bare hands. You can't do such a thing in your own natural strength. It takes supernatural strength to do it.

Although such an act could be done by the power of God, He doesn't act like this for show. God wasn't involved in this. It was a manifestation of the power of Satan. Satan can do supernatural things, so don't get alarmed when you see him doing something supernatural.

Understand this: Everything that is supernatural is not from God. Many people think that just because something is supernatural, it is of God, but that is not true. If you have any life of God in you at all, you will know right away which power is operating.

The man who lived among the tombs had often been bound with fetters and chains, but he broke them apart. "...Neither could any man tame him. And always, night and day, he was in the mountains, and in the tombs, crying, and cutting himself with stones" (Mark 5:4–5).

We would say he was out of his mind, and we would lock him in a padded cell in an insane asylum. We'd keep him there so he couldn't hurt someone else or himself. But because they didn't have such facilities in those days, he wandered around in the cemetery, living in tombs and caves, crying, cutting himself, and acting crazy.

A Matter of Choice

Now notice verse 6:

MARK 5:6
6 But when he saw Jesus afar off, he ran and worshipped him.

This doesn't say the devil told him to run to Jesus. The man cried out as he ran. The demons in him didn't want to go to Jesus, but they couldn't keep him from going, either. The man was crazy—demon possessed—but when he saw Jesus, he saw his deliverance, and he ran to Him and worshipped Him. That's why he got delivered.

If you read the other account of this in Matthew's Gospel, you will see there were two men there (Matt. 8:28). It doesn't say anything about the other man running to Jesus. The other man didn't get delivered, but the man who ran to Jesus did.

Even when you're demon possessed and crazy, you can make a decision to go to Jesus for help, and this man made that decision. Whomever you yield yourself servant to obey, his servant you are. The crazy man was in the worst condition anyone could be in, yet he could still run to Jesus and get delivered.

MARK 5:7

7 [He] cried with a loud voice, and said, What have I to do with thee, Jesus, thou Son of the most high God? I adjure thee by God, that thou torment me not.

That's not man talking. That's the devil in him talking out of him.

Jesus' Reaction

MARK 5:8

8 For he said unto him, Come out of the man, thou unclean spirit.

See how simple it is? You don't have to argue with the demon-possessed man; you don't have to persuade him; and you don't have to knock him down, sit on his chest, thump him, and do all sorts of things people say you have to do. Just speak the Word of God from your heart!

MARK 5:9–10

9 And he asked him, What is thy name? And he answered, saying, My name is Legion: for we are many.

10 And he besought him much that he would not send them away out of the country.

This is not a formula of how to get people delivered. Jesus asked this question so we would know how unlimited the power of God is to deliver. This man had thousands of devils in him—a legion. Some people will tell you there are as many as 6,000 in a legion. I would say a legion is probably 2,000.

MARK 5:11–12
11 Now there was there nigh unto the mountains a great herd of swine feeding.
12 And all the devils besought him, saying, Send us into the swine, that we may enter into them.

Those devils would rather have a body of *any* sort than be without one. They would rather have a pig's body than have no body! Things aren't so good in the kingdom of darkness if they'd come to this!

I'm not encouraging you to hold a pity party for the devil, but things are not good in his realm, either for him, his principalities, powers, and rulers of darkness, or anyone who gets involved with them.

A legion of devils were living in one man's body. They knew they were going to have to leave, and they begged Jesus' permission to go into the pigs' bodies.

I always say that Jesus killed two birds with one stone in this incident. He got the man delivered—and He got rid of all the pigs, which the Jews were prohibited from eating.

MARK 5:13
13 Forthwith Jesus gave them leave. And the unclean spirits went out, and entered into the swine: and the herd ran violently down a steep place into the sea, (they were about two thousand;) and were choked in the sea.

That's why I believe a legion was 2,000 in number. The remainder of this verse says that the pigs ran into the water and drowned. *Not even a pig wants to live with a devil in him!* But some people do.

When People Refuse Deliverance

Some people don't want to be delivered. And if they don't want to be delivered, you can't do one thing for them except pray that their attitude will change!

You can make intercession for them that God will grant them repentance and they will see the light and change what they want, but you can't do a thing against their will to deliver them. If you've ever tried, you know you can't.

MARK 5:14–15
14 And they that fed the swine fled, and told it in the city, and in the country. And they went out to see what was done.
15 And they come to Jesus, and see him that was possessed with the devil, and had the legion, sitting, and clothed, and in his right mind: and they were afraid.

They didn't say, "Hallelujah, this man has been delivered!" No, they were *afraid* of what they found. Often natural people are afraid of God's power when it appears, because they don't yet know that God uses His power to do good. They're afraid of it, but they shouldn't be.

They've got everything backwards. They think that good is evil and evil is good. That's a bad situation to be in.

I want you to understand that the demon-possessed man had the ability to make a choice, and he made the decision to run to Jesus and get delivered. The other man didn't choose to be delivered, and he remained the way he was.

Miracles in Manila

Brother Lester Sumrall had a similar experience with a young man in the Philippines. He had a great revival that centered on a young woman who was delivered from a demon infestation in her life.

She was in prison when Brother Sumrall met her, because she was doing such wild things. She was just as crazy as the man who lived among the tombs. When Brother Sumrall spoke the Word of God to her, she got delivered.

Out of that great miracle of deliverance, thousands of people were saved, and Brother Sumrall founded a church in Manila. The church grew rapidly, because more miracles like that happened.

As a result, an American Navy retiree came to Brother Sumrall. He told Brother Sumrall that his 10-year-old son was demon-possessed, and he asked Brother Sumrall if he could help them.

The boy's actions were really "far out." The boy's father told Brother Sumrall, "This boy is so demon infested that he can be sitting in the middle of the living room, and all of a sudden he'll disappear. He's gone—just like that! And sometimes he doesn't come back for three or four days. Then, all of a sudden, he just reappears in the middle of the room."

How would you like to raise kids who are doing things like that? It's hard enough when you can watch them.

The boy wanted to be helped, so they took him to Brother Sumrall, and Brother Sumrall helped him get free. The boy and his parents got saved and filled with the Spirit and became members of Brother Sumrall's church.

A Surprising Discovery

Brother Sumrall had a great interest in learning more about the boy's experience. He waited until the boy had grown in the Lord for about six months. Then he asked the parents if he could talk to the boy about the things that had happened to him before his deliverance.

Notice he waited until the boy had grown some in the Lord. He didn't ask right away. His motive wasn't simply to satisfy his natural

curiosity; he genuinely wanted more knowledge about demon pos-
session. You've got to be led by the Spirit when you deal with cases
like this.

The parents gave Brother Sumrall permission to question the boy.

He asked the boy, "When you were possessed by the devil that had
control over you, did you always do what he told you to do?"

That 10-year-old boy said, "No, I didn't."

"What did the devil do if you didn't do what he told you to do?"

The boy replied, "He *whimpered.*"

That is a little different from what we would think, isn't it? Often
we think that someone who is demon possessed is terrorized, driven,
and tormented by a big, bad devil. But all this devil could do when the
little boy wouldn't obey him was whimper and bawl about it!

If that 10-year-old boy didn't want to do what this powerful spirit
wanted him to do, all he had to do was say, "No, I'm not going to do
it," and he settled that matter!

You *can* make a choice. God has given you the ability to make
choices.

How much more of a choice do you have when you're free in
Christ?

How much more of a choice do you have when you've been delivered from all the power and authority of darkness, and you're walking
in the light of God's Word? When this is true of you, you can make
every choice you face in life correctly.

3

The Origins of Satan

The nastiest critter of all is the devil himself. He is not even admired in his own realm.

Some people think he still has a great anointing on him, but he no longer resembles what he was when he had an important role in heaven. If you could see him as he is now, you would be appalled and amazed, because he is not anything like what he tries to make people think he is.

He operates by deception, by masquerading, and by overcoming you through your senses, if you allow him to. However, if you are not ignorant of his devices, he can't get away with it.

If some little puppy, just weaned from his mama, came up and grabbed you by the cuff or the hem of your skirt, you wouldn't be too disturbed, would you? He doesn't have any teeth yet; not enough to hurt you, anyway. He only has his milk teeth.

The same is true of the devil. He will be the least of your problems if you understand the truth about him as revealed in the Word; and if you know you are living in Christ and you are indwelt by the Spirit of the living God.

The biggest problem in your life will be overcoming the tendencies of your flesh. Many things that people blame the devil for are nothing more than their own flesh taking over and dominating them.

Of course, when you let your flesh dominate you, the devil will get involved and make it seem 10 times worse than it really is, but that's because you are deceived. If you are walking in the flesh, you are deceiving yourself and giving place to the devil.

Satan's Origins

Let's begin our study of Satan by looking at his origins. It is important to understand where and how he originated.

The being we know as Satan or the devil was created by God, because everything that was created was created by God. John 1:3 says, *"without him* [Jesus, the Word] *was not any thing made that was made."* Although God created everything, many things have been corrupted, and God didn't do that.

In the beginning, this being that we know today as Satan was created by God for His purposes; specifically, he was created by the Lord Jesus Christ Himself, because the Bible says, *"Without him* [Jesus Christ] *was not any thing made that was made."*

The first chapter of Colossians bears that out. Verse 15 says of Jesus, *"[He] is the image of the invisible God, the firstborn of every creature,"* or the preeminent being in the whole universe.

The passage continues,

COLOSSIANS 1:16–17
16 For by him [Jesus] were all things created, that are in heaven, and that are
  in earth, visible and invisible, whether they be thrones, or dominions, or
  principalities, or powers: *all things were created by him, and for him*:
17 And he is before [or above] all things, and *by him all things consist.*

From Lucifer to Satan

So Jesus created Satan, but he wasn't called Satan when Jesus created him. He was an angelic being called Lucifer. Many translations call him Daystar, Bright Shining One, Star of the Morning, Light Bearer, and so forth. The *King James Version,* however, translates the word as "Lucifer" in Isaiah 14:12.

Don't call the devil "Lucifer" today. He is no longer anything like he used to be, and he doesn't act anything like he acted before God threw him out of the kingdom of heaven, so why should we call him a name that no longer relates to what he is? Lucifer is what he *was;* it's not what he *is.* And he hasn't been that way for a lot longer than you can imagine.

His names today are many. In the Word of God, he is referred to by more than 40 different names. Why do you suppose God would call him more than 40 different names? God has a purpose for it; He doesn't do anything without a purpose. The names Satan is called reveal a great deal about his devices, so we will study them as we go along.

Knowledge of Two Realms

Ezekiel 28 refers to the devil's origins and how he became what he is today.

The first 10 verses refer to his working in a human being, *the prince of Tyrus,* but verses 11 and 12 say, *"Moreover the word of the Lord came unto me, saying, Son of man, take up a lamentation upon the king of Tyrus."*

There are two realms we must be knowledgeable about. The first realm is *the kingdom of this world.* The second is the spiritual kingdom, *the kingdom of darkness* that is above the kingdom of this world. It manipulates the kingdoms of this world, seeking to control them. It will, too, if we believers don't do anything about it. You and I are the only ones who can do anything about it.

Who has dominion in the earth? We do. God depends upon us to do something about this situation.

The Underlying Cause

Every time you see anything evil happen in the natural realm, the underlying cause is from the kingdom of darkness.

That's why the Word of God tells us that we do not wrestle with flesh and blood but with principalities, powers, the rulers of the darkness of this world, and spiritual wickedness in high places (Eph. 6:12).

The kingdom of darkness is where the true cause of evil things is, and that's where you have absolute dominion. Therefore, that's where you can cut off evil situations or circumstances if you understand who you are in Christ. But you can't do it by wrestling with it in the natural realm.

Many well-intentioned people try to change things in the natural realm, but because they do little in the way of faith and prayer, they can't accomplish what they want to.

Full of Wisdom, Perfect in Beauty

Returning to Ezekiel 28, verse 12 says, *"take up a lamentation upon the king of Tyrus, and say unto him, Thus saith the Lord God; Thou sealest up the sum, full of wisdom, and perfect in beauty."*

Although God is referring to Satan and Satan's origins here, He is not referring to the way Satan is today. He is referring to the way Satan was created, and He says so plainly in verse 13: *"Thou hast been in Eden the garden of God."*

God said Satan sealed up the sum of creation, was full of wisdom, and was perfect in his beauty. In other words, he perfectly reflected the glory of God's creation the way God made him.

God says Lucifer was in Eden, the garden of God. In this case, however, "Eden" is another name for the earth. The Garden of Eden, mentioned in Genesis, was the place God created for Adam and Eve. So this is not referring to Satan being in the Garden of Eden to tempt Adam and Eve.

When he showed up in the garden, he didn't appear there full of wisdom or perfect in beauty, and he didn't seal up the sum of creation.

He appeared there as the fallen being he is today, and he tempted Adam and Eve, drawing them away from obeying God.

The Anointed Cherub

The Eden that is referred to here in Ezekiel 28, the garden of God, is something that *predated* the creation story found in the Book of Genesis. Satan existed before the creation we read about in the first chapter of Genesis. He existed, first of all, as the cherub that is mentioned in Ezekiel 28:13, where God said:

EZEKIEL 28:13

13 ...every precious stone was thy covering, the sardius, topaz, and the diamond, the beryl, the onyx, the jasper, the sapphire, the emerald, and the carbuncle, and gold: the workmanship of thy tabrets and of thy pipes was prepared in thee in the day that thou wast created.

All these precious stones represent or symbolize something Lucifer possessed—something he was, some ability he had, some appearance God gave him, or some responsibility that God invested in him. And he had many responsibilities.

Note that man was not yet created when all this happened. Lucifer held a central place among the created beings, the angelic beings, in his time. In fact, he was the *mimshach.* Verse 14 says, *"Thou art the anointed cherub that covereth; and I have set thee so."* In Hebrew, the word translated "anointed cherub" is *mimshach,* a word that is only used once in the Bible, here in reference to Lucifer.

If Lucifer was this central being that had responsibility from God over the order of creation, we may assume he was of the highest order of creation. He was wonderful in his order of creation, a marvelous being to behold.

He had tremendous responsibilities and tremendous abilities to fulfill those responsibilities God invested in him. He held a central position in relation to all the other angelic beings, above them and responsible for them in many ways.

Lucifer's Musical Ability

The scripture also says that Lucifer had the workmanship of "tabrets and pipes," which are musical instruments. Some translations don't translate these words as "tabrets and pipes," but I think the *King James Version* translated them accurately.

"Tabrets and pipes" reflect that Lucifer had great musical ability. God gave him that ability to worship and praise Him and to lead the other angelic beings in unified praise and worship of God. That musical ability was vested in him so God would be magnified in the presence of all the created angelic beings. That was one of his functions.

But Lucifer fell. He became something far different from what God had created him to do and be. He still has musical ability, but it has been corrupted. He still uses music, but it isn't to worship and magnify God. *Today, Satan uses music to magnify himself and draw men away from God.*

When you listen to any kind of music, you'll know right away which kind it is—you will have an inward witness to it—and you won't need anyone to tell you if it is edifying and God-like or the exact opposite, originating from Satan.

The Tainted Realm of Music

When you think of satanic music, you probably think of acid rock, rock 'n' roll, or something like that, but the whole realm of music— even popular music and classical music—has been infested.

Of course, not all classical music is satanic. Much of it has been made into church music, and it will bless you when you listen to it, because it was inspired of God in the first place. However, there are classical pieces that were inspired by the devil, and you only have to listen to them for that to be apparent.

Arturo Toscanini (1867–1957) was a great conductor who immigrated to this country from Italy and led great symphony and philharmonic orchestras. He refused to play the music of a certain composer, because every time he did, something dreadful happened to someone in the orchestra!

After it happened so frequently, common sense told Toscanini that he shouldn't play that music anymore, so he just quit playing that composer's music. I used to mention who it was, but I'd get arguments from people who claimed, "That guy wasn't so bad."

I'm just telling you what Toscanini said. He knew from experience that every time one of his orchestras played this man's music, someone died, was injured, or had a horrible accident. It happened over and over again, because playing this music gave a place for devils to operate in!

Addicted to Music, Drugs

When I started in the ministry, I worked with kids who had serious drug problems. Most of them were addicted—and nearly every one of them was addicted to rock music. Often that's how they got addicted to drugs. I'd rather get someone off heroin than rock music. It's easier.

Acid rock music is strictly satanic, but it isn't the only music that is. Even country and western music is infected.

A current joke asks, "If you play a country and western music record backwards, what do you get?" The answer is, "You get your pickup back, your hound dog comes home, and your mother-in-law leaves."

I like country and western music. I used to be a real "picker and grinner" myself. I played it and sang it for years, and some of the songs I sang told me exactly why I was in the mess I was in before I got saved.

"Born to lose, I lived my life in vain..." Go around singing *that* phrase over and over again, and see what happens in your life.

"Why don't you love me like you used to do? Why do you treat me like a worn-out shoe? My hair's still curly and my eyes are still blue. Oh, why don't you love me like you used to do." Sing *that* and see what happens in your family relationships!

An Invitation to Satan

When you confess things like that over and over again, you're giving the devil a wide-open avenue to come in and attack you. And that's just the tip of the iceberg.

Satanic music lyrics are full of pathos. They describe terrible things that are always happening to people. "There stands the glass. Fill it up to the brim, till my troubles grow dim, brother. I'm on my way." You're on your way, all right—your way to destruction!

As you sing those lyrics continually, they become part of you, and you're giving the devil a highway to destruction in the middle of your being.

Again, it isn't only acid rock, rock 'n' roll, country and western, or classical music that is affected; the whole musical realm is affected.

You will know immediately when you start listening to it which kind of music it is, because you have the testimony of the Holy Spirit in your spirit. He will warn you. And when you check out the words to some of the songs in your hymnbook, you will find very bad unbelief expressed even there.

Many think they can dabble with satanic music and it won't hurt them. Don't fool yourself! You're not so tough in the natural that you can expose yourself to something that gives Satan access to you and you will remain unaffected. It gives him access to your life.

When you are warned not to participate in a certain kind of music, leave it alone. Don't listen to it. Don't give Satan access to you!

The Perfection of Creation

Ezekiel 28:14 continues, *"Thou art the anointed cherub that covereth; and I have set thee so: thou wast upon the holy mountain of God."* That means Lucifer was in the kingdom of Heaven. "The holy mountain of God" means the kingdom of Heaven.

Notice the phrase *"and I have set thee so."* God gave this anointed cherub his central place. God gave him that responsibility, and He created him with the ability to fulfill it.

Verse 14 concludes, *"thou hast walked up and down in the midst of the stones of fire."* That means "in the midst of the angelic company"!

Now carefully notice the beginning of verse 15: *"Thou wast perfect in thy ways."* Did God ever create anything with a flaw in it? Did He create Lucifer as a being that had a propensity for evil that he just couldn't overcome? No, He created Lucifer *perfect* in all his ways. Everything God ever created was entirely perfect.

The Origin of Sin

Verse 15 says, *"Thou wast perfect in thy ways from the day that thou wast created, till iniquity was found in thee."* In other words, you might say that *iniquity or sin originated with the devil* as he disobeyed something and became something that God did not create him to be.

Some people say, "It tells you here that the devil was full of pride." Pride was the result of what he did, but pride wasn't why he disobeyed. If he had been full of pride, he wouldn't have been perfect, would he?

God didn't create Lucifer full of pride, and he didn't wake up full of pride one day. Lucifer did something that caused pride to enter into him, and we are going to find out what that was.

Today Satan is trying to draw us into doing the exact same thing that caused pride to enter him! And he is working a lot harder on believers than he is on people in the world of sinners. Why? Because he already controls the world; they're all wrapped up!

This passage describing Satan's origins was written *"for our admonition, upon whom the ends of the world are come"* (1 Cor. 10:11), so we will not make the same mistakes others have made, and so we will not be drawn away by the mistake that Lucifer committed and did not repent of.

How Iniquity Was Found in Lucifer

Ezekiel 28:16 reveals how iniquity was found in Lucifer: *"By the multitude of thy merchandise they have filled the midst of thee with violence, and thou hast sinned."*

The word "merchandise" to us means physical, natural things. When you go into a store, you say it's full of "merchandise." But you need to understand the way the word is used in this passage.

It is the same word translated "traffick" (traffic in modern English) in verse 18: *"Thou hast defiled thy sanctuaries by the multitude of thine iniquities, by the iniquity of thy traffick."*

"Traffick" and "merchandise" are the same Hebrew word. It means actions, goings, and doings as well as the devil's thinking process.

Lucifer began to look at all the things he had been given. He began to focus his attention upon his abilities, his blessings—all the things God had given him in every realm in which he existed—and he began to value these *things* that God gave him more than he valued the God Who gave them to him. He began to idolize them!

How To Make an Idol

That's how the devil became what he is today! That's what he's trying to get us to do—make an idol. You can make an idol out of anything. You can even make an idol out of things that are *good.* You can value things more highly than you should.

You can make an idol out of healing. You can value healing more highly than you value the Healer. You can value prosperity more than you value the God who prospers you.

You can value power more than the God Who gives it. That's what Lucifer did. He began to value his power, his authority, his dominion, himself, the way he was, his abilities, and his possessions more highly than he valued the God Who gave them to him. When you've done that, you've made an idol out of the things God gave you.

Idols are nothing more than anything taken beyond what God gave them for. You may say, "In this modern world, we don't make idols! We don't fall down before carved totem poles or something and worship them."

Primitive peoples who worship things like that mostly act out of ignorance. Actually, we act 10 times worse than they do! Furthermore, not everyone who worships idols today does it in ignorance. Many do it fully understanding what they are doing. They value their positions of authority, their power, their wealth, and so forth, and they don't want any part of God, because they think they will have to give up their idols if they do.

Modern Idolaters

I've witnessed and testified of Christ to people whose answer to me was, "I've got a lot of money. My family's doing fine. I've got several cars, a boat, and a big house. What do I need Jesus for?"

That's sad, isn't it? They are idol worshippers. They are worshipping things much more than ignorant people worship a wooden or a metal idol they have made.

In fact, our generation is the worst generation of idol worshippers that has ever lived! We put more things in a place of more importance than any other generation—and religious people are the *worst* offenders. By "religious," I mean people who are trying to make themselves acceptable to God.

Christians don't need to do that. *The very act of trying to make yourself acceptable to God is probably the worst idol that can be worshipped.* And religious spirits are some of the hardest to deal with.

Why Sin Spreads

Ezekiel 28:16 shows where sin began in Lucifer: *"By the multitude of thy merchandise they have filled the midst of thee with violence, and thou hast sinned."*

Lucifer valued something more highly than he valued God! *Sin began there,* and it spread. Sin doesn't confine itself to one area. *If you submit yourself to sin in any area of your life, it will soon infest and ruin every area.*

Verse 16 concludes, *"therefore I will cast thee as profane out of the mountain of God: and I will destroy thee, O covering cherub, from the midst of the stones of fire."*

God said He would remove Lucifer from the angelic company—and He did. God said He would cast him out of the kingdom of God—and He did. If you read Ezekiel 28 in the original language, you will see there isn't any strict tense to it.

You can see plainly from the Word that God has *already* cast Lucifer out of the kingdom of Heaven. He is no longer in the kingdom of Heaven, and he can't get back into it, because God's Word cast him out.

Your Place of Safety

I think this is a great revelation. It helps you know that *you have a place where Satan can't get to you.* Although he can get to you because you are a human being, and he has access to you through the natural parts of your life—your mind, thinking, and emotions—he cannot get to you through your spirit.

Satan isn't "super spook." He doesn't have some big end run that he can surprise you with in the middle of your spirit. He can't get there! God cast him *out* of the kingdom of Heaven. You, on the other hand, were born *into* the kingdom. You're *in;* he's *out.*

You were born into God's kingdom. You are a created being who has come out of darkness into light. Satan was in light and chose darkness. Now he is in total darkness. There is no light in him, and he can't get to where light is.

Did darkness ever drive out light, even in the natural realm? If the lights are on in a room, can darkness drive out the light? You can turn the lights off, but darkness can't replace the light. It *always* works the other way. Light replaces darkness, but darkness does not replace light.

John 1:5 says, *"And the light shineth in darkness; and the darkness comprehended it not."* The word "comprehend" means "overcome."

Lucifer's Journey From Light to Darkness

You have been born into the kingdom of heaven, the kingdom of God's life and light. God, who is light, lives in you, in your spirit. He has come to make His home and abode in your spirit. Darkness cannot enter there. Darkness can't drive the light out.

"But I heard someone say it could."

So what? It isn't true. Ten thousand people could say it could, but that doesn't make it true. Darkness has never driven out light, and it never will. It cannot. It's not possible. Of course, light can be turned off. No one is going to argue that point, but why would you want to turn off the light in your life when you know what will happen if you do?

We have seen that God said to Lucifer in Ezekiel 28:16, *"I will destroy thee, O covering cherub, from the midst of the stones of fire."* You could just as well translate it, "I *have* destroyed thee." God has already done it. Satan is not wandering in and out of the kingdom of Heaven today. He is out—by the Word of God!

So you can read this, *"I have destroyed thee,* O covering cherub, from the midst of the stones of fire. Thine heart was lifted up because of thy beauty" (vv. 16–17).

Lucifer began to think more highly of himself than he ought. He began to value the things he had more than he valued God, his Creator, who gave them to him.

Verse 17 continues, *"thou hast corrupted thy wisdom by reason of thy brightness."* Lucifer once was the wisest of all created beings, yet he did something absolutely foolish. You can't go from one viewpoint like this to the opposite in one little step. Lucifer's fall must have happened progressively.

The Process of Overcoming

You know God. God lives in you. If you start to think or do wrong, what does God do in you? He warns you; He doesn't watch you head toward destruction and never say a word.

The minute you start to do wrong, the conscience part of your spirit and God Himself in your spirit warn you. I'm sure God warned Lucifer, but he didn't heed the warning.

Perhaps you never ignored such a warning, but I did once, and I have lived to regret it. I'm still regretting it 30 years later. I'm still eating the fruit of having my own way.

You ask, "Why don't you just overcome it?" I am, but some things aren't overcome easily. Some things take longer. And some of the things you set in motion by your actions cannot be reversed without harming other people. God isn't going to do that simply because you are repentant.

Yes, God will forgive you. He will cleanse you of unrighteousness as soon as you repent, but the consequences of your actions won't fall away because you repented. The consequences of your wrongdoing continue, but you can overcome them, because God will show you how to overcome them. A process of overcoming is going on in each of our lives.

Let's look at a simple example. Two people commit fornication and have a child. That means they have a responsibility to that child that will last for the rest of their lives. That child is their responsibility before God, whether or not they marry and whatever else happens. That consequence of their actions doesn't disappear once they repent of what they did wrong. There are many examples like this.

Some things you can repent of quickly and overcome the consequences. In other cases, consequences happen immediately after you disobey. Those are the things that don't disappear simply because you want them to.

The Foolishness of Solomon

Satan corrupted his wisdom because of his "brightness," the simple glory of his being as God created him. Other figures in the Bible did the same thing, and Satan led them to do it.

The prince of Tyrus mentioned in Ezekiel 28:2 did it. Solomon, the world's wisest man, became the world's biggest fool! When you read the Book of Proverbs, you see wisdom upon wisdom upon wisdom from Solomon, inspired by the Spirit to be recorded so we would have access to it and be blessed by it.

But read the Book of Ecclesiastes and tell me what you see. Solomon wrote both books. He wrote Ecclesiastes later in life, after he had corrupted his wisdom. In it you will see flashes of revelation and flashes of hopelessness.

You will see Solomon in despair, saying, *"Vanity of vanities, saith the Preacher, vanity of vanities; all is vanity"* (Eccl. 1:2). Is life really all vanity? If it's all vanity, what are we doing here?

But all of life is not vanity. Solomon wasn't telling the truth. You say, "It's in the Bible, isn't it? It *must* be the truth." It's the truth that Solomon wrote it, but what he wrote wasn't the truth.

Don't forget, you will also find things the devil said in the Bible, but that doesn't mean what he said is true. You will find things other despairing men said in the Bible. It doesn't mean it's the truth. It was written for our admonition, that it might teach us something, so we won't make the same mistakes they made.

"All scripture is given by inspiration of God" (2 Tim. 3:16), yet I've heard people quote that and say, "All scripture is *inspired* of God." No, it isn't. There are a lot of things in the Bible that *aren't* inspired of God. It's all given to us by the inspiration of God, but all of it is not God talking.

The devil talks in the Bible. Is that God talking? Men talk in the Bible. Is that God talking? That's where people make a mistake. Although all scripture is given by the inspiration of God, it is not all God speaking Himself. But it is all holy scripture, and it is all prof-itable for our admonition. Every bit of it admonishes, teaches, and instructs us.

Restricted to Earth

Returning to the origins of Satan, God said in Ezekiel 28:17, *"I will cast thee to the ground."* Where is that? Here on the earth! God cast Lucifer out of the kingdom of Heaven down to earth. Here is where he is, and here is where he must remain, because that's the Word of God.

God can't say, "I'll cast you down to the ground" by His Word and then turn him loose any time the devil wants. That would be changing God's Word.

So Satan is restricted to earth. Here, in the earth and its atmosphere, is where he must stay. This is the realm he affects today.

You may wonder, "Why did God put us here on Earth? Why didn't He put us on Mars, Venus, or someplace where the devil *isn't?*"

Do you know why God put you here? To overcome what the devil did—sin, rebellion, and all that they bring. How can you overcome what he did unless you're where he is? Can you overcome what he did where he *isn't?* No, you can't. You wouldn't know what he did, you wouldn't know how he operates, and you wouldn't have any contact with him.

How Creation Was Defiled

God further tells Lucifer in Ezekiel 28:17–18, *"I will lay thee before kings, that they may behold thee. Thou hast defiled thy sanctuaries by the multitude of thine iniquities."*

All things that are defiled today in the order of creation—things that are fallen, things that are under the curse—are defiled by the devil's iniquity and by Adam's having followed in the devil's way.

"By the iniquity of thy traffick" (v. 18). In other words, by the multitude of Lucifer's "merchandise." It's that same word again, valuing what God gave more than the God Who gave it.

Verse 18 continues, *"therefore will I bring."* That sounds like it is in the future tense, but it's not. It could have been translated, *"I have brought forth* a fire from the midst of thee, it shall devour thee, and I will bring thee to ashes upon the earth in the sight of all them that behold thee."

How do you properly behold the devil today? With your own eyes? No, you've probably never seen him. I haven't, and most people haven't, so you'll never behold him that way. But you can behold him. How? Scripture reveals him to us.

God said He doesn't want us to be ignorant of the devil's devices (2 Cor. 2:11), so scripture shows us his true condition today.

Dealing With the Devil

Back in the late 1960s, when Brother Kenneth Copeland was getting started in his teaching ministry, I heard him say, "You know, it's time we jerked the wraps off the devil, because he's going around convincing church people by and large that he's something he isn't at all; that he's some big, bad dude you can't do anything about."

Yes, you can do something about him. You can do *anything* about him that needs to be done—but you have to do it in the Spirit realm. You cannot do it in the natural realm!

The devil has come in the natural realm and spoken to church people who weren't living in the Spirit enough to recognize they were being approached this way. He told these people he's so big and bad, they ought to be afraid of him. And they believed him!

Brother Kenneth E. Hagin once attended a meeting of ministers, and they were talking about physical problems people had. Brother Hagin said he knew he was healed by Jesus' stripes, nothing was going to change that, and he had the ability to live in divine health because of what Jesus had done.

Other ministers warned him, "Oh, I wouldn't say that very loud if I were you. The devil might hear you!"

And Brother Hagin said, "That's exactly the dude I *want* to hear me. That's who I want to hear it the most. He needs to hear that I *know* it."

Fully Persuaded

When the devil knows you know the truth, his access to you is blocked. It's not God Who needs to hear it. God is already persuaded of His Word, and He doesn't need you to persuade Him.

And you are not *persuading* the devil; you are *commanding* him. You are the one who needs to be persuaded. God has given you all you need to be fully persuaded. He has made you able to partake of the inheritance of the saints, the Word of God.

The Word of God sets you free. It delivers you. It liberates you from fear, bondage, and everything else the enemy has ever brought. Basically, it sets you free from the fear of death and all the bondages that result from that fear. You need not be afraid of death anymore.

"If you're face-to-face with death, you sure feel like you're afraid of it!"

Yes, you do. I've been there. I know. You do feel like you're afraid, but that doesn't mean you *are*. Your body can feel afraid, and you—the man on the inside—are not afraid at all.

An Unholy Terror

"All they that know thee among the people shall be astonished at thee: thou shalt be a terror" (Ezek. 28:19). Christians are the only people who know the devil for what he is, and we know him because of or through the Word of God.

Believers are not held in bondage any longer by the devil's devices. We know him as he really is, because we know who set us free. We run our race, keeping our eyes on Jesus, the Author and the Finisher of our faith (Heb. 12:2).

"Thou shalt be a terror." The devil shall be a terror to mankind—to the world out there, to people or sinners who don't know the truth about him—but it's the other way around when you know the truth.

The devil is terrified of you, because there is no weapon he can form against you that will prosper. He knows he can't run over a Spirit-filled believer who is walking in the light of God's Word.

So if you are walking in the light of the Word of God—walking in the Spirit, in other words—he can form a weapon against you, but it will not prosper or work against you.

Satan Is Already Defeated!

Isaiah 54:17 says, *"No weapon that is formed against thee shall prosper; and every tongue that shall rise against thee in judgment* [including the devil's] *thou shalt condemn."* You will show it to be faulty, non-working, and non-productive. How will you do that? By believing the Word, no matter what the devil says or does.

"This is the heritage of the servants of the Lord, and their righteousness is of me, saith the Lord." Satan can't invade that. He can't remove it. He can't do anything to change it, as long as you know that.

Believe me, whatever area of life you're in—whatever you're called to do—you are going to have to deal with this fallen creature the devil, and you're going to have to do it successfully to obey God.

I don't think there are "deliverance" ministers as such, and those who say they are aren't the only ones who can get rid of the devil. Every believer needs to be able to keep the devil in the place of defeat Jesus put him in. We don't have to try to defeat him; he has already been defeated!

Terminated!

"Thou shalt be a terror, and never shalt thou be any more" (Ezek. 28:19). The devil's got a termination date! God's got a retirement plan for him. God doesn't have one for you, but He's got one for him.

One of these days Satan is going to be totally "retired" in a place called the Lake of Fire. When that occurs, there will no longer be a memory of him in you or in any part of God's creation. God is able to do that.

Today, however, you need to remember what God says about the devil, because he is still able to affect you in this world. When is the time to overcome? It's now. This is the opportunity you have been given to overcome.

There will be no opportunity to overcome after you leave this world. Why? Because as a saint you will go out of this world to go to Heaven, where God is. The devil isn't there, so you will not have to overcome him there. In Heaven, there will no longer be any world system against you or any more problems with the flesh for you to overcome. They'll be gone, too.

If you're ever to overcome the world, the flesh, or the devil, where are you going to do it? Right here. When? Right now, in this lifetime. There won't be any opportunity to overcome in the next life. There will be nothing left to be overcome in the next life.

If you want to have the title "Overcomer" applied to you, do it now, because if you don't, you will lose out on a blessing you could have had for all eternity. It's not that you won't be in eternity; it's just that you won't be all that God made you to be in eternity if you don't overcome now. Now is the time!

Don't wait until later. Don't think you can glide and slide through life and then make up for it somehow later on. There won't be any way to make up for it later on. The devil will be retired. You won't even remember there *was* a devil. I'm looking forward to that day!

Satan Can't Hurt You!

In Luke 10:19, Jesus commissioned His disciples to go out and preach the Gospel. They went, healed the sick, raised the dead, and did everything else He told them to do. They returned rejoicing.

Verses 17 and 18 report:

LUKE 10:17–18
17 And the seventy returned again with joy, saying, Lord, even the devils are subject unto us through thy name.
18 And he said unto them, I beheld Satan as lightning fall from heaven.

Verse 19 is very important. Jesus said, *"Behold, I give unto you power."* The word really is "authority." Like Brother R.W. Schambach says, "I give you POWER!" He makes it sound like it's exploding when he says it.

"I give unto you power to tread on serpents and scorpions, and over all the power of the enemy: and nothing shall by any means hurt you."

No device Satan has and nothing he does can hurt you!

4

Far Above Temptation

Make this confession as you read:

"I am a child of the living God. Jesus is my Lord.

"I run my course and race with my eyes fixed on Him, expecting to receive something from Him.

"He never lets me be ashamed. He always fulfills His Word. He keeps every promise He makes, watches over His Word, and performs it for me.

"No matter what I face, nothing is bigger than He is. Jesus is my Elder Brother. He is with me. I live in Him, move in Him, and have my being in Him.

"Day by day I receive strength to run my race, because I am looking unto Him.

"Thank You, Father, for your great mercy and grace by which You have saved me.

"Thank You for your full salvation. Thank You that You made me aware of it and made me able to receive all that You have done, in Jesus' Name."

That's the blessed condition believers live in. Next, we're going to look at the cursed condition suffered by those who dwell in the kingdom of darkness.

Remember, Lucifer was cast out of the kingdom of God, but you were born into it. He is out, and you are in—in Christ! Satan lives in darkness, and you live in light. He lives in disobedience, and you live in obedience.

We could list a thousand contrasting things like that. Always think in terms of living in God, His Word, and His power. You live, move, and have your being in Christ.

As we look at what Satan has done, let's start with Isaiah chapter 14, where we clearly see the contrast between Satan and his forces and the Lord Jesus Christ. Verses 12–14 say:

"I Will, I Will, I Will"

ISAIAH 14:12–14

12 How art thou fallen from heaven, O Lucifer, son of the morning! how art thou cut down to the ground, which didst weaken the nations!

13 For thou hast said in thine heart, I will ascend into heaven, I will exalt my throne above the stars of God: I will sit also upon the mount of the congregation, in the sides of the north [where God sits]:

14 I will ascend above the heights of the clouds; I will be like the most High.

"I will, I will, I will, I will, I will!" Five times in this passage, Lucifer said, "I *will* do this. I *will* do that." Contrast that with Jesus' prayer in the Garden of Gethsemane. He said, *"Nevertheless, not my will, but thy will be done."* There wasn't anything wrong or evil with His will. He was the perfect, spotless Son of God.

He said, "Whatever I see the Father doing, that's what I do; and whatever I hear the Father saying, that's what I say." He would not exercise His will contrary to the will of the Father. That's the way you and I ought to be.

The Repairer of the Breach

Jesus was the very Son of God, begotten to come into the world as the man Christ Jesus to save us from what Satan had done.

Iniquity began with Lucifer, so Jesus came to save mankind from that iniquity and to repair the breach that existed between God and man as a result of Adam's sin of disobeying God.

The Word says that Jesus reconciled us to God. "Reconciliation" means "to remove the difference." That means He removed the difference that existed between God and us. The difference was sin. It's no longer there. Aren't you glad Jesus removed it?

Anyone who believes what Jesus did will receive salvation and be reconciled to God. But, like anything else, you've got to *believe* it in your heart and *confess* it with your mouth in order to *receive it.*

What Is Faith?

As you live in this world, your thoughts, thinking, and soul are being renewed if you are a *doer* of the Word. However, *hearing* the Word alone doesn't renew your mind. Hearing the Word brings faith.

What is faith? Faith is confidence in Jesus that results in *acting on* the Word of God. Believing the Word isn't simply saying, "Yes, I believe that." That's only mental assent. Believing the Word is speaking from the word in your heart, but *there must be a corresponding action for that to be faith.* So faith is saying *and* doing what the Word says.

In His parable about building your house on the sand or on the rock, Jesus taught about people who hear and then do or do not do what they hear. The wise man is the one who hears and does what he heard. That's what believing is.

Faith is not just hearing, but *faith comes by hearing.* If you don't *hear,* you won't be able to *do.* It is the doing that renews your mind. *"He that doeth truth cometh to the light,"* John 3:21 says. Proverbs 16:3 also says something concerning this: *"Commit thy works unto the Lord, and thy thoughts shall be established."*

How to Make Proper Decisions

Remember, you think in the realm of your soul, and your feelings are in the realm of your soul, not your spirit. Your will is also in the realm of the soul. That's where you make decisions. Thus, the ability to make decisions is in the realm of the soul. The soul must be renewed for you to make proper decisions.

If you commit your works to the Lord—in other words, be a doer of the Word—your thoughts, your mind, and your soul will be established in God's Word. But not until you are a doer of the Word.

Some people run from place to place, thinking the next time they hear the Word of God, it's going to straighten things out for them, but it never does. You can hear the Word indefinitely, but it will never straighten out the way you think or act until you put it into practice in your life.

So it's not hearing the Word again that will change things for you; it's doing what you have heard. However, you do need to keep hearing, because faith comes by hearing—present tense. It doesn't come by *having heard*—past tense. Continuing in the Word of God ensures that you are living in faith and continuing to apply what you have heard.

Jesus had a mind that agreed with God. When He said, "Not my will but thine be done," that's what He meant. He had already prayed, "If there be any other way, let this cup pass from me" (Luke 22:42).

There was no other *way* under Heaven whereby men could be saved. There was no other *name* under Heaven whereby we could be saved. So Jesus became sin for us. He had to drink the cup.

Raised From Death to Life

You will notice that when God raised Jesus from the dead, He raised Him *"Far above all principality, and power, and might, and dominion, and every name that is named"* (Eph. 1:21).

And Ephesians 2:1, 6 says, *"And you hath he quickened, who were dead in trespasses and sins. . .and hath raised us up together, and made us sit together in heavenly places in Christ Jesus."*

At the very moment Jesus was raised from the dead, you and I were also raised from the dead with Him!

You say, "I wasn't even born then!" No, but God still raised you from death to life then. God can do things like that. Even before you exist, He can provide for you spiritually, and that's what He did. He knew by foreknowledge you would live on Earth and you would trust in Jesus.

In fact, God has known you from the foundation of the world, because you are a believer. He knows everyone who will believe, and He has provided them with everything they need as an inheritance in order to be overcomers.

In the Process

That means that the process of renewing the mind removes you from that place where your will is always done, because God's will becomes more important than your own will.

Believe me, it's a process. You're going to have test after test in this area, for it never stops. In this lifetime, you are in a process of submitting your will to God.

You will never get to the point where you can say, "I finally got it all submitted." When you think that, you're about to find out what isn't submitted But God is patient. I'm certainly glad He's patient with me.

He's satisfied if you are in the process. He's not concerned about whether or not you're going to finish it. He knows you will if you continue in the Word. Why do you suppose the Bible says so much about continuing in the Word? Because it's necessary for you to finish your course and race. It's necessary for you to stay in the Word and fully attain the place God put you in.

Little Foxes

After Lucifer turned and went the other way, he said things that were impossible. For example, he said he was going to take God's place. That was not possible, but by the time he said it, he was really deceived. And who deceived him? He did! He deceived himself.

How do you deceive yourself? By disobeying God. If you walk in the opposite direction to what the Word of God says in any area of life, you are deceiving yourself.

Sometimes people say, "Oh, well, it's just a little thing. It won't make any difference." What does the Word say about that? It says that the *little* foxes, not the big ones, spoil the vines.

If you allow little things to be contrary to God in your life, sooner or later they will become big things, and they will spread. Little foxes spoil the whole vine, not just the branch that is affected at the moment.

Ignorant Statements

Lucifer made ignorant statements. Did he accomplish any of the things he bragged about? No. There are some things you can say a thousand times, but they will never come to pass.

As Brother Kenneth E. Hagin says, "You can go out in your garage and call yourself a Cadillac, but you're not going to become one."

God has set and established certain laws in motion that you can't change, even if you say something contrary to them 10,000 times.

The law of gravity isn't going to change just because you don't want to abide by it at the moment, is it? It is a natural law, and if it stopped, we'd all fly off the face of the earth and become "unguided missiles," going we know not where. That law must continue, or we would not be able to remain here on earth.

The law of gravity can be overcome temporarily, but I don't know of anyone who ever overcame it permanently. Airplanes overcome gravity temporarily, but when the airplane runs out of fuel, the law of gravity takes over, and down the airplane comes. While it has fuel, while the engines are running, and while the wings are still attached, the airplane overcomes the law of gravity because *higher laws* apply. However, the law of gravity doesn't cease just because the airplane is flying. It's still there.

Overcoming the Law of Sin and Death

It's like that with the law of the spirit of life in Christ Jesus and the law of sin and death. You have been put in a position in the law of the spirit of life in Christ Jesus by virtue of your new birth.

Living by faith overcomes the law of sin and death, but it's still there. Continue to walk in the law of the spirit of life in Christ Jesus, and apply it in your life. Continue in the Word of God, running your race and looking unto Jesus. If you don't do these things, the law of sin and death will start nipping at your heels again.

The law has not gone away. It's still there. It's a law that God set in existence. Although you have overcome it in Christ, it doesn't mean it has been set aside. It's still in existence.

If I choose today to sin and disobey God, He cannot prevent me from doing it other than by persuasion. He cannot and will not force me not to. Why? Because He has given me dominion in the earth. He has also given me—like every other spirit being He ever created—free choice or free will. All of us must make correct choices in order to live blessed lives.

Seeing the Deceiver

Lucifer made wrong decisions. I know God warned him, because I know what God does to me when I start to think wrong: He warns me right away. But Lucifer didn't heed God's warning. He went his own way *until iniquity was found in him.* Sin began with Lucifer, and it has spread from him to many other created beings, including one-third of the angels.

After Lucifer bragged about all the things he would do, this is what actually happened to him, according to Isaiah 14.

ISAIAH 14:15–16

15 Yet thou shalt be brought down to hell, to the sides of the pit.

16 They that see thee shall narrowly look upon thee, and consider thee, saying, Is this the man that made the earth to tremble, that did shake kingdoms.

"They that see thee" are the ones who will see Satan correctly, and the only way to see him correctly is to see him in the Word of God. He is a deceiver. He goes around masquerading as something he's not to try to deceive people.

If you try to deal with Satan with your own human understanding, you will fail every time. He has to be dealt with by revelation knowledge—and revelation knowledge comes by your knowledge of God's Word.

So those who see Satan properly in the Word of God and understand by revelation what he is really like shall consider him and say, "You mean this is the one that caused all the trouble?" If you see him as he is from your position far above him in Christ, you will see him correctly.

Verse 17 continues, *"That made the world as a wilderness, and destroyed the cities thereof; that opened not the house of his prisoners?"*

The Earth Before Adam

As you read and meditate on these things, you will realize that there was an order of creation on earth before Adam was ever created.

It says in Isaiah 45:18 that God made the earth to be inhabited. He made it not *tohu* and *bohu,* Hebrew words that are translated as "without form and void" in Genesis 1:1–2, which says, *"In the beginning God created the heaven and the earth, and the earth was without form and void."*

God did not create it that way. It became that way. The word "was" can be translated "became," and it is translated "became" more than 60 times in the Old Testament.

So the Earth was inhabited, but it was inhabited by *spirit beings,* not human beings. Adam was the first *human being,* the first man. There were none before Adam.

If you study how the words *tohu* and *bohu* are used in the Old Testament, you will find they are translated in many different ways. But "without form and void" is probably the best way. Sometimes they are translated "wind and confusion," "wilderness," or "like spiritual wilderness."

That's the way the earth became because of Satan's rebellion against God. God didn't make the earth that way; He made it to be inhabited. If He made it to be inhabited, it *was* inhabited, but the beings that inhabited it joined with the devil in his rebellion against God. That's why they're in the condition they're in today. Satan and these beings have all been judged.

Both John's Gospel and Matthew's Gospel say that Satan has *already* been judged and cast out of the kingdom of God; he is not waiting to be judged.

The final step of that judgment is to separate him and everything that pertains to him to the Lake of Fire. In that place, they will be eternally separated from everything that is God-like. We won't remember them. It doesn't mean they won't be there; it just means we won't have any contact with them any longer. I'm looking forward to that day!

How the Wisest Man Became Foolish

Earlier we mentioned how Satan had influenced King Solomon to become foolish by disobeying God's Word. Solomon evidently reached the place where he thought that he could decree God's laws to the nation of Israel as the head of that kingdom and require the people to obey them—but he himself was exempt from God's laws!

Have you ever known people like that? We've seen them in the Church, haven't we—much more than we should. Such people preach the truth to other people and require them to live it, but they don't want to live it themselves for some reason.

Solomon was reared in David's home. He was taught the Jewish Law from the time he was a child. One of those commandments prohibited the Jews from intermarrying with people from other nations. Another told him that he should have only one wife; he should not live in an adulterous relationship; and fornication was against the law for him.

Just to show you how merciful God is and how far He goes to keep us from doing wrong, He appeared to Solomon twice and personally told him not to make the mistake of marrying wives from other nations.

Solomon's Folly

What did Solomon do? He married 700 wives from other nations and brought all of them to Israel. And he didn't just bring them; he brought all their idols with them! What did he do with the idols? Did he put them away in a back room? No, he put them right in the Temple of God! That wasn't very smart was it? And in addition to his 700 wives, Solomon had 300 concubines. He had 1,000 women!

In his day, Solomon was the wisdom of God personified in man. People came from all over the world to see him and be blessed by his wisdom. Wisdom only comes from God, so it was godly wisdom.

Yet that wise man disobeyed God, not once or twice, but 1,000 times in the same area God had warned him against. Evidently, Solomon thought he was above what God wanted. He came to the place where he was deceived by disobedience.

God's plan is for one man and one woman to marry. That's the plan, the only plan, that makes anyone happy.

I always say that the world's wisest man in that case became the world's biggest fool. How did he think he could keep 1,000 women happy?

A Foolish Prince

Solomon wasn't the only person affected by disobedience to God's Word. Ezekiel 28 tells us about another man, the earthly prince of Tyre, who was affected by Satan in the same way. He disobeyed God and was led into the same thing—idolatry—that Satan is trying to lead us into today.

Why was the prince an idolater? Because the devil misled him to value created things more than he valued his Creator. Ezekiel 28:1–3 says:

EZEKIEL 28:1–3
1 The word of the Lord came again unto me, saying,
2 Son of man, say unto the prince of Tyrus, Thus saith the Lord God; Because thine heart is lifted up, and thou hast said, I am a God [that's the height of deception], I sit in the seat of God, in the midst of the seas; yet thou art a man, and not God, though thou set thine heart as the heart of God:
3 Behold, thou art wiser than Daniel.

Daniel had wisdom 10 times greater than anyone in the Babylonian Empire! Where does wisdom come from? From God. This man was greatly blessed with godly wisdom.

Blessings Bring Responsibilities

When you have been the recipient of great blessings from God, responsibility accompanies those blessings. God expects you to be responsible for those great blessings and to use them the way He intended, not some way your flesh desires.

If they are no longer a *blessing,* they become a *curse.* The same thing that will bless you will curse you when you make an idol out of it! It's called "covetousness" in the New Testament. Twice it says that covetousness is idolatry. Give heed to this.

Ezekiel 28:4 reveals what the Prince of Tyrus did wrong. This is what made him go astray: *"With thy wisdom and with thine understanding thou hast gotten thee riches."* God does not give you wisdom and understanding so you can heap up treasures on earth for yourself. There is a much greater, more noble purpose than that, and you will be blessed in fulfilling that purpose.

What did Jesus teach His own disciples? *"Seek ye first the kingdom of God, and his righteousness; and all these things shall be added unto you"* (Matt. 6:33). However, if you seek things first, this promise isn't going to work for you. It isn't going to be a blessing, even if you get the things. Instead, it's going to be a curse.

Why Blessings Are Withheld

God doesn't give great earthly treasures to people who won't know what to do with them, because He would cause them to stumble if He did. If they get these things, they didn't get them from Him.

God doesn't have a get-rich-quick plan, either. Some people seem to think He does, but Proverbs 28:20 says otherwise: "A faithful man or woman shall abound with blessings." That's because this person seeks first the kingdom of God and His righteousness. That's his purpose on earth—not to heap up treasures—but to seek God and His righteousness and do His will.

The passage continues:

PROVERBS 28:20–22
20 ...but he that maketh haste to be rich shall not be innocent.

21 To have respect of persons is not good: for for a piece of bread that man will transgress.

22 He that hasteth [or is in a hurry] to be rich hath an evil eye, and considereth not that poverty shall come upon him.

God doesn't want you to be prospered in the natural realm faster than your soul prospers, because if you do, your flesh is going to control it. But as your soul prospers, you will be able to keep your body under subjection, and then God can trust you with more and more.

A Channel of Blessing

As the saying goes, "God will get it *to* you if He can get it *through* you." God doesn't want you to keep heaping up things for yourself. He wants you to be a channel of blessing, and He will bless you abundantly if you are able to pass that blessing on like God made you to do.

It's more blessed to give than receive. Why do you suppose God said that? Because the more you give, the more you receive! You can't outgive God; neither can you turn it around. It's not more blessed to receive than it is to give. God didn't give you faith just to get things for yourself. There are many other reasons why He gave you faith.

"He that hasteth to be rich hath an evil eye, and considereth not that poverty shall come upon him." This is what the prince of Tyre did not understand. What did he do with his wisdom?

EZEKIEL 28:4–10

4 With thy wisdom and with thine understanding thou hast gotten thee riches, and hast gotten gold and silver into thy treasures:

5 By thy great wisdom and by thy traffick hast thou increased thy riches, and thine heart is lifted up because of thy riches:

6 Therefore thus saith the Lord God; Because thou hast set thine heart as the heart of God;

7 Behold, therefore I will bring strangers upon thee, the terrible of the nations: and they shall draw their swords against the beauty of thy wisdom, and they shall defile thy brightness.

8 They shall bring thee down to the pit, and thou shalt die the deaths of them that are slain in the midst of the seas.

9 Wilt thou yet say before him that slayeth thee, I am God? but thou shalt be a man, and no God, in the hand of him that slayeth thee.

10 Thou shalt die the deaths of the uncircumcised by the hand of strangers: for I have spoken it, saith the Lord God.

This prince, like King Solomon, corrupted his own wisdom. He used it for wrong purposes; he used it for something contrary to the Spirit, contrary to seeking God, contrary to seeking God's kingdom and righteousness.

When he did that, he corrupted his own wisdom. Although his wisdom was greater than Daniel's, it became corrupt, just like Solomon's. *Corrupt wisdom isn't a blessing anymore.*

It is God's will to prosper you—but in the way outlined in the Word, not in some other way. It is God's will to prosper you *as your soul prospers*—not as everything your flesh desires.

The Problem With Power

Power can corrupt a person. People shouldn't have too much authority or power to exercise before they are ready for it. That's why God said, "Don't give positions of authority to a novice" (1 Tim. 3:6). The novice will misuse power. He will use it according to his flesh. Then he will suffer for having done so—and so will everyone who is influenced by him!

One of the New Testament scriptures written to us about covetousness is First Timothy 6:10: *"For the love of money is the root of all evil."* Verses 8–10 say:

1 TIMOTHY 6:8–10

8 Having food and raiment let us be therewith content.

9 But they that will be rich fall into temptation and a snare, and into many foolish and hurtful lusts, which drown men in destruction and perdition.

10 For the love of money is the root of all evil.

Paul didn't say money is the root of all evil, did he? He said *loving it* is. If you love money and what money can buy, you have made an idol out of it.

The passage continues in First Timothy 6:10–11:

TIMOTHY 6:10–11
10 For the love of money is the root of all evil: which while some coveted after, they have erred from the faith, and pierced themselves through with many sorrows.
11 But thou, O man of God, flee these things; and follow after righteousness, godliness, faith, love, patience, meekness.

These people coveted money and what money can bring—power and all the things that come from having lots of it.

Fight Covetousness

Paul warned, *"Fight the good fight of faith, lay hold on eternal life, whereunto thou art also called, and hast professed a good profession before many witnesses"* (1 Tim. 6:12).

Look further at Ephesians 5:3–5 to see how this warning is consistent throughout the New Testament:

EPHESIANS 5:3–5
3 But fornication, and all uncleanness, or covetousness, let it not be once named among you, as becometh saints;
4 Neither filthiness, nor foolish talking, nor jesting, which are not convenient: but rather giving of thanks.
5 For this ye know, that no whoremonger, nor unclean person, nor covetous man, who is an idolater, hath any inheritance in the kingdom of Christ and of God.

People who have nothing can be covetous. And people who seemingly have everything are still covetous! Their flesh lusts after what they haven't got. When your flesh is lusting, you're never satisfied. You can't satisfy lusts of the flesh. Lusts of the flesh are things of man taken beyond what God made them for.

Making the Right Choice

When you're thirsty, you should give your body something to drink, but you don't need to give it 10 gallons. You don't need to drink a case of beer or something like that. There are choices to be made in this area. You need to be constrained by what you know about thirst.

Thirst is a good thing, but taken beyond what it is meant for, it becomes a lust, and it begins to control people. It is the same with every other drive the body has.

Paul wrote that while some coveted after these things, they forsook their inheritance. The most amplified of all the Ten Commandments in Exodus 20:17 is, *"Thou shalt not covet."* Then God went on to tell them what not to covet.

Why do you suppose He amplified this commandment? Because covetousness is common to man; it is something the enemy tries to introduce into your life in many ways.

In Luke 12:15, Jesus said, *"Beware of covetousness."* Colossians 3:5 says, *"Mortify* [put to death] *therefore your members which are upon the earth."* It literally means to put covetousness to death by starvation. Don't feed it. Don't allow it to control you.

Don't let lust affect how you make your decisions. If there is something you are having difficulty with in your life, don't put yourself in the position where it is even a temptation to you.

Flee Temptation

When I operated a program for young people who had drug problems, we kept them on the property. We didn't let them roam around in town. Why? There were drug dealers in that town, so we separated our young people from temptation for that period of time in their lives.

If you break a leg, what do you need to walk with? A crutch. You can't walk on a broken leg without damaging it. You need a crutch.

However, after your leg has been healed for a while, you don't need to use that crutch anymore. You need to walk on the leg again.

Of course, you cannot forever isolate yourself from every temptation there is, but you can cut yourself off from anything that is really troubling you. Don't let it happen. Don't even get in a place where it could happen.

I know people who were like I was. They were boozers. And when they got saved, they wanted to go down to the bar and win all the people there to the Lord. Instead, they ended up going back to drinking! Why? Because they were brand-new babies, and when they got to the bar, they got tempted beyond their means to resist. God did not put them back in there; their own human thinking and human compassion led them there.

I've seen similar situations where people wanted to go back to something they'd been delivered from, but they didn't go back at the direction of God. They went back because there was a need.

Needs do not dictate what you ought to do. There are more needs in this world than you can ever meet. God will lead and guide you to the needs He wants you to meet. A need is not a call.

Changing Your Thinking

How can you control your mind? If you'll say what God says, if you'll speak the Word of God out loud, just like when your thinking is troubling you, it will change your thinking.

"How long do I have to keep saying it?"

Until your thinking changes. Generally, it doesn't take long.

That's what putting the Word of God in your mouth will do for you. Speak it out loud out of your mouth, and it will change the way you're thinking. But when you're tempted by ungodly thoughts, don't get condemned. Satan shoots fiery darts at *everyone's* mind. No one can escape. It's a temptation that is common to man.

You don't have to take it! The problem comes when you take an evil thought, meditate on it, and turn it over and over in your mind. Jesus said, "You have committed adultery if you even think about it." You don't have to think about it.

If a thought comes to your mind, it doesn't mean it's in your *heart.* It's just in your *mind,* and you can deal with it there. That's the place where you can drive it away.

Speak what the Word says. Say, "No, devil, you can't put that on me! I'm a new creation in Christ Jesus. I'm born again. I'm the righteousness of God in Christ. I have a renewed mind." Say what the Bible says. Don't say what the devil is saying to you.

Modern Idolatry

"Mortify therefore your members which are upon the earth; fornication, uncleanness, inordinate affection [affection beyond what it ought to be], *evil concupiscence* [a mind that thinks of contrary things all the time], *and covetousness, which is idolatry"* (Col. 3:5).

Here again in Colossians we see that covetousness is idolatry. It's just the same as making an idol, bowing down, and worshipping it. This is not different from pagans who worship idols, although I think that many of the modern forms of idolatry are worse than that, because they're not done ignorantly.

In First Timothy chapter 3, Paul describes the attributes a bishop should have, but they would apply to anyone in a position of leadership in the church; especially a pastor.

The qualifications call for a person who is *"Not given to wine, no striker, not greedy of filthy lucre; but patient, not a brawler, not covetous"* (1 Tim. 3:3). Thus, a leader in the church needs to be a person who has overcome covetousness and is no longer dictated to by the lusts of the flesh.

Such scriptures are common in the New Testament. Another is Hebrews 13:5: *"Let your conversation* [or manner of living] *be without covetousness; and be content with such things as ye have."*

People who are discontent all the time are covetous. If you are content with what you have, God will bless you and will multiply grace, peace, and knowledge of Himself to you. Beyond that, He will multiply all kinds of material blessings to those whose minds are being renewed.

It seems that the apostle Paul warned against covetousness to everyone to whom he wrote. Jesus has much to say about it. Peter and John addressed the issue in their epistles. Anything that is so frequently discussed must be a common problem that needs to be overcome.

So it is not unusual to be tempted this way; it's normal. But you are far above all that temptation in Christ!

5

Rebellion in Heaven

When a person who has authority or great influence commits sin, it always influences other people adversely. The leader who does wrong is not the only one who suffers as a result of his or her actions.

When Jonah ran away from God, his action affected everyone who was on that ship with him.

When Lucifer, the created angel who was the day star, rebelled against God and became what he is today, he influenced other created beings. Some followed him in his rebellion, and others did not.

In the twelfth chapter of Revelation there is a pause. It's almost like God were saying, "Time out! Let's stop and look at why things are happening the way they're happening and why all of this is being fulfilled. Let's stop and think about all the things the prophets have said from time immemorial. Let's see if it's coming to the place where I said it would; let's see if their prophecies are coming to pass as I said they would. "

Revelation chapter 12 shows us the majesty of God and how He is able to perform His Word and keep it perfectly. Even if it takes thousands of years, it will come to pass just as He said. Of course, with God that's not so long. A thousand years is like a day to Him, and a day is like a thousand years (2 Peter 3:8). So if this order of creation has been here for 6,000 years, and it's going to be fulfilled in 1,000 more years, altogether that is like a week to God!

Two thousand years ago, the Age of Grace began. As God sees it, that's only two days ago, so it's not such an awesome thing to Him.

To us it is, and it should be. It should be awesome to us to see how God is able to fulfill everything He has said.

Past Influences

In Revelation 12, references are made to many things that happened long ago, some things that will be happening at this time, and other things that remain to be fulfilled in the future.

If I asked one of my students, "How did you get here today," he would probably reply, "I got in my car and drove here from home." Then I would say, "Let's go back further into the past. What influenced your being here now? There were a lot of things, weren't there?"

In your own lifetime, you can think of many things that have happened to you, things you have done, and decisions you and others have made that affected you. You could go back as far as you are able and trace your ancestry. All of this had something to do with your being here today. And, of course, what Jesus did 2,000 years ago had a lot to do with your being here today.

Great Wonders in Heaven

There are many things in Revelation chapter 12 that have to do with what is being fulfilled and completed at the end of time as we know it. The first verses speak of a great wonder in Heaven:

REVELATION 12:1–2, 5

1 And there appeared a great wonder in heaven; a woman clothed with the sun, and the moon under her feet, and upon her head a crown of twelve stars:
2 And she being with child cried, travailing in birth, and pained to be delivered. . .
5 And she brought forth a man child, who was to rule all nations with a rod of iron: and her child was caught up unto God, and to his throne.

There is no doubt about who that man child is. It was Jesus brought forth through the believing remnant in every covenant God established with mankind to bring forth His salvation in the earth.

The woman brought forth a man child who was to rule all nations. In verse 5 you can see what that has to do with the Body of Christ as well as Christ Himself: *"And her child was caught up unto God, and to his throne."* Then it speaks about that woman being persecuted greatly in the end times.

Return to verse 3: *"There appeared another wonder in heaven; and behold a great red dragon, having seven heads and ten horns, and seven crowns upon his heads."* That dragon is Satan when he rebelled against God, and when he became what he is now.

Verse 4 says, *"His tail drew the third part of the stars of heaven, and did cast them to the earth."* This means a third part of the angelic beings, because stars symbolize angels. You'll see this over and over again throughout scripture.

How the Devil Works

Lucifer drew a third part of the angelic company with him. He deceived them. He drew them away from God. But He didn't stand up one day and announce, "I've become the devil. How many of you want to follow me?" The angels wouldn't have done that. He drew them away the same way he tries to draw you away—*subtly.*

He doesn't announce his presence to you, saying, "Hello, I'm the devil. I'm here to steal your health." You wouldn't give it to him, would you? He doesn't say, "I'm here to steal your finances." You wouldn't give him anything if you knew who he was and what he was up to.

He comes subtly. At some point you realize that the devil is trying to work on you. Then you rebuke him and take care of the situation. But sometimes when a problem begins, you won't understand immediately that the devil is behind it, because he works subtly.

Your attention must be captured *spiritually* to recognize what is going on. It is by the Spirit, by the Word of God, that you recognize the devil's workings; it's not just by natural information.

Sometimes, however, you can see it naturally. When a tornado blows your house down, that's pretty good evidence that something was going on that was not caused by God! However, there are other ways the devil approaches you that are much more subtle as he tries to draw you away. That's how he tempted and approached the angelic company.

Seeds of Dissatisfaction

Years ago, there was a popular teaching that seemed to attract a lot of followers. They believed that Lucifer, Michael, and Gabriel were all archangels, and each had one-third of the angels under his control. When Lucifer rebelled, this teaching said, Lucifer's third group of angels *had* to go with him. That's not true!

Every spirit being God ever made has a choice and the ability to choose. Those who followed Lucifer *chose* to do so. The angels were deceived, but they made their choice. How did Lucifer deceive them? If you look at the devices he uses today, you can see how he worked then.

As he became what he is, Satan drew some of the angels away by planting seeds of dissatisfaction in them. These were not major seeds, such as, "Are you really getting what you ought to get from God?" No, they were little ideas that wouldn't necessarily jump out at them right away as being wrong. He started to work on them the same way he did on himself.

One-third of the angels—the third part of the stars—followed the dragon, and they were cast to the earth. When this happened, it happened in Heaven as well as on earth, and it happened in the heavenlies around the earth.

Job's Dilemma

Job was asked questions he couldn't answer. God appeared to him and asked him about many things. All Job could answer was, "I don't know."

God was trying to make him realize that he didn't know everything; in fact, he didn't know much at all! When Job finally came to that realization, he repented and was sorry for the things he had said against God. He said those things because that's what he thought.

That's still true today, as you will find out when you minister to people. What they don't know can be easily dealt with by hearing the truth. But it takes longer—it takes the renewing of the mind—to change what they think they know.

Job didn't know everything he thought he did. God said to Job, "Job, where were you when all the morning stars sang together and all the sons of God shouted for joy? All of the created beings were in unity and harmony and there was no sin, period" (Job 38:2–7).

How long was it like that? It all happened long before Adam was ever created.

When Christians say the earth is only 6,000 years old, they are actually speaking ignorantly, because their own Bible teaches them that the earth is a lot older than that. The Bible doesn't say how much older, but it could have been millions of years older.

Lucifer in Eden

We know this for sure: The order of creation we live in began about 6,000 years ago—but that doesn't mean the earth is only 6,000 years old.

I believe that Lucifer, as that great archangel, had a responsibility in this earth before he fell. It says in Ezekiel that he had been in Eden, the garden of God. "Eden" is another word for earth; it wasn't the Garden of Eden inhabited by Adam and Eve. So Lucifer had been on the earth before Adam and Eve, because the earth was created long before the Genesis account.

Lucifer's rebellion is referred to in Revelation 12:7. Lucifer's tail drew the third part of the stars (or angels) out of Heaven. It was a great wonder. This is not a reference to a future event. It has already happened, as we saw in Ezekiel and Isaiah.

War in Heaven!

REVELATION 12:7–8

7   And there was war in heaven: Michael and his angels fought against the dragon; and the dragon fought and his angels,

8   And prevailed not; neither was their place found any more in heaven.

This is plain that it's not something that is going to happen in the future. Do you think Heaven is populated by the devil and his angels today?

That doesn't make sense. Do you think God coexists with the devil? Do you think He sits on His throne and the devil sits across the room on his throne? Of course not! God doesn't coexist with evil.

God has dealt with Lucifer's rebellion; Lucifer has already been judged. He was not only cast out of the place called Heaven; he was cast out of the whole kingdom of Heaven as well. That's why he is here on the earth today.

Reprobate Beings

He caused one-third of the angelic company to willfully follow him in rebellion against God. Jesus taught in Matthew 25:41 that hell was originally created only for Satan and his angels: *"Depart from me, ye cursed, into everlasting fire, prepared for the devil and his angels."*

Ephesians 6:12 also refers to the beings that were cast out and were judged because they had become reprobates.

There are beings in the earth today that we call demons or fallen angels. Are they the same? I don't think so, but they all became fallen spirits during the rebellion that Lucifer caused.

Ephesians 6:10 says, *"Finally, my brethren, be strong in the Lord, and in the power of his might."* Say this out loud: "I am strong in the Lord, and in the power of His might. If R.W. Schambach were to say that, he'd say, "And in the POWER of His might. When he says that, you know it's power! There's no doubt about it.

Then, Ephesians 6:11 says, *"Put on the whole armour of God, that you may be able to stand against the wiles of the devil."* What is the whole armor of God? It is explained to us in the next verses. All the parts of the armor are nothing more than other words for the Word of God.

Levels of Demons

By the Spirit of God living in you, applying that Word, you will overcome the devil in everything he does. There is no created being you can't overcome.

Some demons are low-life, low-level demons. Some have different levels of ability. Others have a little more ability to bother you, and some have a great deal more ability to bother you. We don't ordinarily come into contact with those that have a great deal more of ability, because there aren't that many of them.

Paul encountered one of the strongest demons on several occasions. He called him "the messenger of Satan" (2 Cor. 12:7). The word "messenger" is *angelos,* the same Greek word that is translated "angel."

The powerful demon that dogged Paul's steps caused whole cities to riot against him! It stirred up all kinds of persecution wherever Paul went.

In Acts chapter 19, Luke describes an incident that happened in the city of Ephesus. The demon stirred up the silversmiths, the copper-smiths, and others who made money making idols against Paul. They all went to the city's famous amphitheater and hollered for two hours, "Great is Diana of the Ephesians!"

Overcoming Powerful Evil Spirits

You can't get a whole city to go to a certain place and yell for hours in your own strength. It takes something beyond your natural ability to cause that to happen. Only a powerful evil spirit could cause it to happen.

An angel (or messenger) of Satan in the earth was causing Paul all this trouble, but he overcame it. *"Out of them all the Lord delivered me,"* Paul said in Second Timothy 3:11. He had to learn to do so, however.

At first, Paul wanted God to do something about that devil. He asked God three times that it might depart from him, but God said, *"My grace is sufficient for thee"* (2 Cor. 12:9). In other words, the ability you have to deal with low-life devils is just as effective to deal with bigger ones.

When I mention "low-life devils," don't think you can disdain them, assume you are bigger than they are, or believe you can over-come them simply by thinking less of them.

You must take dominion over them! You must stand on the Word of God and wear the whole armor of God to deal with them, because they work through deception and things you wouldn't have any way of knowing if it weren't for God's Word.

People Aren't the Problem

Ephesians 6:12 says, *"We wrestle not against flesh and blood."* *People are never our problem.* God didn't send people into the world for us to deal with, other than to preach the Gospel to them. We are not here to straighten out everyone who is wrong. In fact, some people will never be straightened out!

Ephesians 6:12 lists devils in ascending order, starting with the lowest level and going to the highest: *"For we wrestle not against flesh and blood but against principalities, against powers, against the rulers of the darkness of this world, against spiritual wickedness in high places"* or in the heavenly places about earth.

Paul writes that we are to put on the whole armor of God in order to deal with all of them. Ephesians 6:13 says, *"Wherefore take unto you the whole armour of God, that ye may be able to withstand in the evil day."* This word could also be translated as "the day of test, trial, or temptation," or even "the day of persecution."

Verses 13 and 14 conclude, *"and having done all, to stand. Stand therefore, having your loins girt about with truth, and having on the breastplate of righteousness."* How do you have righteousness? By knowing and believing the Word of God. The Word is your righteousness.

"And your feet shod with the preparation of the gospel of peace" (v. 15). What is the Gospel? It is the Word of God. God's Word is good news.

Taking the Shield of Faith

"Above all, taking the shield of faith" (v. 16). How can you know when you are in faith? Because you are standing on the Word. The Word is always the foundation for any faith you are standing in.

"Wherewith ye shall be able to quench all [not most of] *the fiery darts of the wicked"* (v. 16). Satan can form a weapon against you, but it won't prosper if you are in faith, and if you are wearing the whole armor of God.

Although Satan fires fiery darts at you, you know that you can quench them. And you know that you are never tested, tempted, or tried above what you are able, because *"God is faithful, who will not suffer you to be tempted above that ye are able; but will with the temptation also make a way to escape, that ye may be able to bear it"* (1 Cor. 10:13). The means He has provided include the Word of God and the Greater One living in you and manifesting Himself to help you.

What the Holy Spirit Does

In John 14:26, Jesus taught His disciples about the coming of the Holy Spirit and what He would do when He came. When He came to indwell them, He would be their Intercessor, Comforter, Helper, Standby, and so forth. Examine the terms "Helper" and "Standby. The Holy Spirit is your Helper. When you need help, He will manifest Himself to help you (John 14:26 AMP).

You can't deal with everything in your own understanding. You need to go *beyond* your understanding. Even though it is *being* enlightened, your understanding isn't *fully* enlightened yet. It is still limited, finite. You aren't to lean on your own understanding; you are to acknowledge God in all your ways.

I acknowledge my dependence on God every day. I like to say, "Lord, I'm dependent on You to be free today and to be able to fulfill your will in my life today. "

When you acknowledge your dependence on God, the Bible says He directs your path. He will see to it that your path is His path. In other words, He will perform His Word for you. He watches over His Word to perform it. He wants you to believe it. He wants you to trust in Him. He wants you to lean on Him.

When you do, no matter what weapon has been formed against you, God will see to it that it won't prosper. Therefore, if someone accuses me falsely, I won't have to hire a lawyer. I'll believe God's

Word, and God will see to it that the accusation won't prosper. If you are falsely accused, remember that. You aren't wrestling with flesh and blood.

A Renewed Mind

You have the shield of faith *"wherewith ye shall be able to quench all the fiery darts of the wicked. And take the helmet of salvation"* (Eph. 6:16–17). What part of your body does the helmet protect? Your head—*your mind.*

These verses refer to the operation of the soul, the part of man that has to do with your feelings, your ability to choose and make decisions, your will, and your thought life.

A renewed mind is what Paul is referring to. The Word of God protects and renews your mind. What word renews your mind? The part you apply, act upon, and put to work in your life.

Paul continues, *"And take the helmet of salvation, and the sword of the Spirit, which is the Word of God"* (v. 17). That sword in Revelation speaks of Jesus in the glorified sense. It says the sword was coming out of His mouth. That's the Word of God that He speaks. When you speak the Word of God, it is the sword of the Spirit, your offensive weapon.

Stay on the Offensive

I like to stay on the offensive. It's better if you stay on the offense rather than the defense. Then you're not just running around quenching fiery darts!

If all you're doing is defending yourself—intercepting fiery darts— you're missing the whole point. Of course, if you see a fiery dart coming, hold up the shield of faith, but also take the sword of the Spirit and give the devil a good jab with it at the same time!

Make him pay! Make him wish he'd never come around you. How can you do that? By wielding the sword of the Spirit, going on the offensive. Let him know he made a bad mistake when he came after you! Let him know, "It is written!"

Satan's whole being is totally in darkness, whereas you are living in light. When you let the light shine forth out of your heart, he hates it. He can't stand light. Why? *Because light drives him out!*

He has no weapon that will prosper against a Spirit-filled believer who speaks the Word of God with power.

The Good Fight of Faith

Paul wrote in Ephesians 6:12, *"For we wrestle not against flesh and blood, but against principalities, against powers."* That word "wrestle" has a special connotation.

Did you ever watch real wrestling? I don't mean professional wrestling, which is more like acting. It's really a big show. Those guys try to impress each other with the size of their biceps as they strut around the ring. If they did that in a real wrestling match, they'd be on their back before they knew it!

On the other hand, if you watch collegiate wrestling or Olympic wrestling—genuine wrestling—you will see that it involves constant effort. Once you begin, you don't stop. You don't draw back. There aren't any time-outs.

When you get on that mat, you wrestle until someone is pinned. Then you get up and begin the next match. You don't say, "Let me catch my breath." About the time you'd do that, you'd be on your back again.

What, then, was Paul saying when he wrote, "we wrestle"? It was to show that there aren't any time-outs in the good fight of faith.

Keep Faith Working

You must keep faith at work in your life, and faith doesn't need a rest. You say, "But all this being in faith tires me out!" Sometimes you feel like you need a rest—and you do, humanly speaking—but you don't need to give your faith a rest.

It's all right to take a vacation, but don't take a vacation from being in faith. Don't think, "I'm going to take a vacation, so I won't read my Bible this week. Don't do it. When you go on vacation, you ought to read *more* than you do the rest of the year, not less.

We saw references to "the rulers of the darkness of this world" and "spiritual wickedness in high places." These are definitely angelic beings that fell with Satan. They are powerful beings that have the ability to influence other spirit beings. They also have the ability to influence human beings who allow them to do so.

Ephesians 6:10 says you are strong in the Lord and in the power of His might. It doesn't make any difference how big or bad the devil or demon is that is opposing you; you are stronger than it is in the Lord and in the power of His might!

The Secret of Paul's Strength

As you will recall, when Paul was tormented by a strong evil spirit, he asked the Lord in Second Corinthians 12:8, "Get this thing off me!" God said, in effect, "Get it off yourself! My grace is sufficient for you. I gave you dominion on earth. Use it. You'll find that it works."

Paul then wrote in verses 9 and 10:

2 CORINTHIANS 12:9–10
9 And he said unto me, My grace is sufficient for thee: for my strength is made perfect in weakness. Most gladly therefore will I rather glory in my infirmities, that the power of Christ may rest upon me.
10 Thereore I take pleasure in infirmities, in reproaches, in necessities, in persecutions, in distresses for Christ's sake: for when I am weak, then am I strong.

Paul acknowledged that he couldn't do anything himself; he was dependent on God's power and ability to deliver and help him. The more you acknowledge that, the more you will see it work in your life. But don't acknowledge your dependency in only one area of your life; acknowledge it in *every* area.

The Holy Spirit has anointed you. He has come upon you for many purposes. Thank God, you have Him to help you overcome your flesh. Thank God, you have Him to help you minister the Word of God effectively. He is upon you to do whatever God called you to do, and He will give you tremendous insights into things that are beyond your own ability and understanding.

Times of God's Judgment

Peter tells about times when God has had to act in judgment, commenting, *"For if God spared not the angels that sinned, but cast them down to hell"* (2 Peter 2:4).

The word translated "hell" is *tartarus*. This is the only time it is used in the Bible. It seems to be the same as the bottomless pit mentioned in the Book of Revelation, and it certainly is a part of Hades or Sheol. It refers to a spiritual place beneath the earth, not a natural place.

I have heard of people who claimed they had dug a deep pit into the earth and opened up hell. They said they heard screaming and hollering.

I don't believe such tales are valid, because if you could dig *into* hell, you could also dig *out* of it. The spirits there are not leaving. They are kept there by the Word of God.

Peter said, *"[He] cast them down to hell, and delivered them into chains of darkness."* The very darkness they are living in chains and binds them. They are reserved unto the final judgment, but their present condition is already a judgment in itself.

The final judgment is when all that is contrary to God and everything that is God-like is finally and forever separated from Him in the lake of fire. That time of God's judgment will come in the future at the great White Throne Judgment.

The Angels' First Estate

Peter called the fallen angels "the angels that sinned." Another reference to God's judgment on the angels is found in the Book of Jude.

Jude described them as, *"The angels which kept not their first estate, but left their own habitation, he hath reserved in everlasting chains under darkness unto the judgment of the great day"* (v. 6).

The angels' "first estate" was holiness. God created all of them holy, just like He had created the archangel Lucifer—the *mimshach*—holy.

As we have seen, when Lucifer became Satan, one-third of the angels followed him in that rebellion and left their first estate. Jude says they "left their own habitation." They left Heaven, deliberately deciding to follow the devil in his rebellion!

I am sure God gave them ample warning to avoid judgment, but they didn't believe Him. The same thing that influenced Lucifer stirred in them, and they left their own habitation and followed him.

Jude compares their judgment to those that came on Sodom and Gomorrah and other places where judgment had to come for human life and God's purpose to be preserved in the earth.

Your Power and Authority

You don't need to be a "super saint" to deal with the devil. Just be aware of who you are in Christ. Every believer who knows this can deal successfully with anything the devil does. We are God's children!

Colossians 1:13 says, speaking of Jesus, *"Who has delivered us from the power of darkness."* That means the power as well as the authority, because it is the Greek word *exousia,* which is generally translated "authority" instead of "power." However, it has to do with both, because authority allows power to operate.

As we just read, Jesus has delivered all of us from the power of darkness. That is true whether you know it or not, and it is true whether or not you act upon it.

Jesus has delivered you from the power and authority of darkness. It has no more power or authority over you, because He destroyed, broke up, and loosened the works of the devil. They no longer have dominion over you. They no longer are able to hold you in bondage unless you let them.

So say, "I am delivered." That's a simple truth. "I *am* delivered; I'm not trying to get delivered. I *am* healed; I'm not trying to get healed. I *am* prospered; I'm not trying to get prospered." What the Word of God says is yours *is* yours!

Redeemed From the Curse

Jesus has redeemed you from poverty, sickness, and death!

This means you are free from all the effects of death and darkness. They are no longer able to hold you in bondage unless you allow them to. All believers are in this place of freedom, whether they know it yet or not.

Many believers who don't know it don't act like they're redeemed or free. They still act like they're in bondage, because they don't know they're free. But they *are* free.

God must be grieved to know that children of His are absolutely free from all the effects of darkness, but they are still bound by it when they don't need to be. Generally, it's because of ignorance.

The Bible says, *"My people are destroyed for lack of knowledge."* That's why Satan is able to destroy some believers. However, those who enjoy an abundance of knowledge of God's Word will no longer be destroyed or in bondage.

Translated Into the Light

God not only delivered you from the power and authority of darkness, but according to Colossians 1:13, He did something else for you: He translated you into the kingdom of His dear Son. This happened *the moment* you were born again.

You were removed from the kingdom of darkness, where you had been spiritually, and you were translated into the light—into the kingdom of Heaven.

Paul wrote in Ephesians 1:21, you are now *"Far above all principality, and power, and might, and dominion, and every name that is named."* Note you are *far* above it, not just *a little bit* above it.

When you know who are and where you are, there is no contest. That's why you can command the devil. You know what your position is. You know where you're coming from. You know you have been elevated in the kingdom of God, far above everything else.

Because you're in that place, you can make this confession: "I live today in deliverance because of Jesus—because of the Word of God— because of the One Who translated me from the power and authority of darkness into the light, into God's kingdom, where I live and move and have my being."

Darkness is around you, and it can have an effect on you. Jesus told His disciples, "You don't need to wash your whole bodies. You just need to have your feet washed." When you're speaking the Word of God, you're washing your own feet.

Often you're delivering yourself from the effects of what is around you in this world. It has an effect on your humanity.

You don't need to go around beaten down by this world's darkness. God gave you the means to overcome it and live above it. You must use the form of doctrine that was given to you. What is that form of doctrine? *Believe* in your heart and *speak* with your mouth.

6

Know Your Enemy

There are more than 200 references to Satan in the Bible, and he is called by more than 40 names. Why do you suppose God gave him so many names? They describe what he does to us, and that's how we learn about his devices.

Each of his names reveals something about what he does, what he's like, or where he's coming from.

Thus, the first reason why we should study the names of Satan is because they are found in the Bible. God put them there. The second reason is, they reveal Satan's present position. Although he will try to convince you he's not like that, his biblical names will show you his present, reprobate, defeated position.

The third reason we study his names is because they reveal his activities; what he's trying to do. The fourth reason for knowing his names is because they reveal his character; what he's like. Some names may show more than one characteristic, but I have grouped them according to their primary meaning.

People ask me, "Aren't you afraid you're going to make people demon-conscious or devil-conscious?" No, God put these names in the Word of God for us to be edified, not to be disturbed by this knowledge. If you get disturbed by information about the devil, it means you are getting something that doesn't come from the Word of God.

The devil is not above trying to deceive you when you are learning what he is like. In fact, that is one of his major functions.

Paul's Admonition to the Church

Ephesians 4:27 says, *"Neither give place to the devil."* The Book of Ephesians was written to us, the Church. It's an admonition to us.

Paul was telling members of Christ's Body, "Don't give place to the devil." The only way he can get a place in your life is if you give him one. Sometimes you do it out of ignorance, and sometimes you do it out of disobedience, but if you give him a place, he'll take it. This implies that you can give him a place if you're not aware of his devices.

If you were walking down the road and an ugly critter came up to you and said, "I want to go home with you," you'd probably go the other way, leaving him behind. If you could see Satan as he really is, you'd react like this with him, too. Don't give him any place in your life!

The Importance of Forgiveness

One way you give the devil a place in your life is by refusing to forgive others.

In Second Corinthians 2:10, Paul says, *"To whom ye forgive any thing, I forgive also: for if I forgave any thing, to whom I forgave it, for your sakes forgave I it in the person of Christ."* By faith, you can forgive others. Even if you don't feel like it, you can still forgive them by faith. Just act on the Word of God, and you will feel differently.

When I need to forgive someone, I hardly ever feel like it. In fact, I can't remember the last time I felt like it! But don't wait until you feel like it to do what you ought to do. You can act in faith. You know you can forgive, because you've been forgiven. You know that ability is in you, because God's love is in your heart, poured out there by the Holy Spirit.

"Not Ignorant of His Devices"

Verse 11 adds that if you don't forgive, you're giving the devil a place or an advantage over you: *"Lest Satan should get an advantage of us: for we are not ignorant of his devices."*

Why aren't you ignorant of his devices? Because of your knowledge of God's Word. His Word teaches you what Satan's devices are. The world does not teach you this. The world doesn't even know what his devices are. That's why they are totally deceived.

So Satan takes advantage of those who are ignorant of his devices. But let's turn this around: If you are *not* ignorant of his devices, he can't take advantage of you. That's why you are studying his names and his devices.

This word "devices" here is interesting. It is the Greek word *noeema*. Everywhere else in the New Testament, it is translated "mind" or "thought." This is the only place where it is translated "devices."

You can say you are not ignorant of Satan's mind or his devices. You are not ignorant of how he operates—and you are not ignorant of the fact that he tries to approach you through your mind and thoughts.

Classified Material

Years ago, I had a job in the Strategic Air Command Headquarters. I worked in a classified vault underground, and the material I worked on was highly classified.

We always had to bear in mind that our enemies would try to figure out everything we did—how we transmitted information and what form it was transmitted in.

Therefore, there was a huge banner about 25 by 6 feet long on the wall. It read, "Know Your Enemy!" If you are conscious that you have an enemy that is seeking to find out what you are doing, or ways to infiltrate and stop your operations, you will be more cautious about what you do. Furthermore, you will understand that anything you do that gives your enemy a place will be a disaster for you.

Your Enemy the Devil

The same is true of your enemy in the spiritual world. If you know Satan, you won't give him a place—you won't let him take dominion over you—because you'll recognize what he is doing as soon as he begins to do it.

Of course, believers don't always recognize the devil the instant he starts doing something, because he doesn't announce his presence.

Satan plants ideas in your mind, and he gets you to think a certain way that doesn't immediately seem wrong—but the more you think like that, the more it "scratches" your spirit the wrong way, and you realize, "That's not God's thought."

Right then is the time to do something about it. You can *replace* thoughts. You can *cast down* imaginations. You can *exalt* the Word of God and put down anything that exalts itself against the Word. If you give God a stronghold in your mind, Satan won't gain a foothold there.

"The Prince of This World"

Some of the names Satan is known by describe his position. In John 12:31, Jesus called him "the prince of this world." That shows he is attempting to rule over this present world system—and in some ways, he is succeeding! As people give him a place, he does succeed.

Verses 30 and 31 say, *"Jesus answered and said, This voice came not because of me, but for your sakes. Now is the judgment of this world: now shall the prince of this world be cast out."*

Jesus was referring to what He came to do: to destroy the works of the devil. In His death and triumphant resurrection, Jesus did that.

He *loosened* you from all the works of the devil. He *disconnected* the hold they had on your life. And He *annulled* what the enemy had done in you as if it had never happened! Realize that Jesus finished the work in His death, burial, and resurrection. It is all done!

Adam delivered authority to Satan in the Garden of Eden. He allowed the devil to rule him and take authority over this world. So Satan really had dominion on earth; dominion that was given to him by man. But Jesus was about to remove it from Satan and return it to believing man, which He did through His own death, burial, and resurrection.

Although Jesus destroyed the works of the devil, it doesn't mean that the devil is no longer at work on earth; it means that his works don't have a hold on you anymore.

Unbelievers' Blindness

That is not true for those who don't believe in Jesus Christ. The devil's got them all wrapped up in darkness, and they do his bidding, whether they know it or not.

I didn't believe there *was* a devil before I got saved, but I was doing his bidding anyway. He will let you think he doesn't exist in order to keep you in darkness. But Jesus said, "The prince of the world shall be cast out."

In John 16, Jesus said, speaking of the Holy Spirit:

JOHN 16:8–11
8 When he is come, he will reprove the world of sin and of righteousness, and of judgment:
9 Of sin, because they believe not on me;
10 Of righteousness, because I go to my Father, and ye see me no more;
11 Of judgment, because the *prince of this world is judged.*

Judgment

Satan is the evidence that there is eternal judgment! A better evidence of this is currently working in you. Your spirit man has already been changed, but there is a process going on in your soul.

God is judging you by the power of His own Word, and He is transforming you into His likeness. He is allowing you to judge yourself by the Word of God. It judges what needs to be judged in your life and changes you into the image and likeness of God's Son.

Satan, the prince of this world, has already been judged. He was cast out of God's kingdom into spiritual darkness here on planet Earth. He is under the active judgment of God's Word.

His title "prince" indicates someone who would rule. The word "world" here is *kosmos*, which means "an ordered system." The word *kosmos* also indicates that the kingdom of darkness is working in that world system.

The kingdom of darkness, a spiritual realm, attempts to rule over the natural kingdoms, and Satan often succeeds wherever humans give him a place.

The word "world" here then refers to both spiritual and natural parts of the world system. Jesus told the most religious people of His day, "You are of your father the devil." Religion is part of that world system. The word "religion" does not refer to faith in God; it refers to man's own idea of how to make himself right with God. The whole system of religion—all the names and varieties of it—is part of the world system, the *kosmos*.

The world system works through lust and pride—the pride of life, the lust of the eye, and the lust of the flesh. That's the means Satan uses to snare and use human beings.

"The Prince of the Power of the Air"

The next thing Satan is called is "the prince of the power of the air." You'll find that in Ephesians 2:1–6:

EPHESIANS 2:1–6
1 And you hath he quickened, who were dead in trespasses and sins;

2 Wherein in time past ye walked according to the course of this world, according to the prince of the power of the air, the spirit that now worketh in the children of disobedience:

3 Among whom also we all had our conversation [manner of life] in times past in the lusts of our flesh, fulfilling the desires of the flesh and of the mind; and were by nature the children of wrath, even as others.

4 But God, who is rich in mercy, for his great love wherewith he loved us,

5 Even when we were dead in sins, hath quickened us together with Christ, (by grace are ye saved;)

6 And hath raised us up together, and made us sit together in heavenly places in Christ Jesus.

In Christ

This is a good place to look back at Ephesians 1:21 and see where that is: *"Far above all principality, and power, and might, and dominion, and every name that is named, not only in this world, but also in that which is to come."* That's the place to which God has translated or raised you to.

You are in Christ in this present world, far above other spirit beings that exist in the kingdom of darkness.

Being the prince of the power of the air reveals limits on where Satan can operate. It's in this world. We've seen additional evidence in Ezekiel and Revelation that he was cast out of the kingdom of God down to the earth.

So Satan's here in this world; he's limited to this realm. He's not roaming all over the universe doing whatever he thinks he can get away with. You might say this world is his prison house! He's imprisoned on this earth, beneath the earth, and in the atmosphere around the earth.

The air defines the limit of what we call the earth's atmosphere. When you look up in the sky and see clouds, lightning, and rain, all that happens within the earth's atmosphere.

The Earth's Atmosphere

When I was flying SR-71's, we flew up really high in that atmosphere. We flew in the top one percent of it, by weight. The air is quite thin there. You've got to go fast to pack enough of it into engines to make them work. That's somewhere in the vicinity of 85,000 to 90,000 feet.

There is some measurable atmosphere up to 150,000 feet. Above 150,000 feet, however, there is not enough air to measure. When you get up to 100,000 feet, you are about 20 miles above the earth. When you get up to 150,000 feet, you are 30 miles high. Above that, you're considered to be in space.

The devil operates in the earth's atmosphere. I'll not try to tell you exactly how many feet he can get up above the earth; that's not important. You're not going to get up there, anyway!

Beyond the Devil's Reach!

However, there is a group of people—astronauts—who went to the moon in the 1960s and 1970s, and all of them had a common experience. They reported that it was very peaceful there. In fact, they named their first moon base Tranquility Base.

Why is it so peaceful on the moon? It could be because the devil isn't there. There is no atmosphere there. The moon is far beyond the devil's realm!

One of my fellow officers in a certain Air Force program went on to become a full-fledged astronaut. His name was James Irwin. He was a Christian then, but he would tell you he was a nominal Christian before he had the experience I am about to relate.

When James walked on the moon, he was on an Apollo mission. His was the mission that took a little lunar rover that looked like a dune buggy strapped to the lunar lander. When they landed on the moon, they unstrapped it and attempted to use it.

That was James' job. When he went to start it, it wouldn't start. It was electrically operated by battery power. The astronauts had two buttons. One was an intercom to talk to each other, and the other enabled them to communicate with the control center in Houston if they had problems. The control center would analyze their problem and give them courses of action to take.

James said he was just about to press the button and ask Houston what he should do, and a Voice on the inside spoke to him very clearly and the Voice said, "Ask Me, and I'll show you what's wrong with it."

Mini Visions on the Moon

James replied, "All right, what's wrong with it?" And he said, "No sooner did I say that, than I had a little vision of what was wrong with the lunar rover." He saw a compartment that contained circuit boards, and on one of those circuit boards there was a flaw that he could correct, even in his spacesuit.

He opened the compartment, pulled up the top circuit boards, looked at this one, and, sure enough, it was exactly like he had seen it. He pressed the board down—it was loose or something—and the rover started right away!

Is God a respecter of men on the moon? No, He is not. He doesn't speak more clearly to men because they are on the moon than He does to us here on earth. James could hear God's voice more clearly on the moon, and he could see things in the Spirit more clearly on the moon, because there is no spiritual interference there.

We live in a place where there is spiritual interference that affects us on the natural level. When we get something in the Spirit, we must perceive it by our spirit. Often, it doesn't come as clearly to our senses as it did to James' senses.

If there was no interference on earth, we would see things immediately in the Spirit, like James did. God doesn't withhold something from us because we're on earth. He speaks to us just as clearly as He did to James.

James said he had another spiritual experience on the moon. When something malfunctioned, he asked the Lord what it was, and immediately he saw what it was in a mini vision. Again, he took care of it.

He said that when he returned to Earth, he hoped that ability would continue, but it didn't. Then he realized something: There is a difference in the spiritual atmosphere on the moon and here on earth!

Clearing Up the Reception

The early radio that I listened to as a boy was AM (amplitude modulation) radio. The radio receiver would receive the radio wave that was transmitted and then translate the sounds in your radio to what you heard. However, summertime thunderstorms could ruin your reception.

Your radio would snap, crackle, and pop, because the lightning—the electrical charge in the atmosphere—added to the amplitude of the transmission and destroyed the "intelligence" that was on it.

I remember listening to ball games at night, when thunderstorms built up. They always seemed to happen at the end of the ball games, and you couldn't hear the outcome of the game.

Then frequency modulation (FM) radio was invented, and it modulated the frequency. A receiver was able to take that modulated frequency, decode it, and let you hear it. The frequency wasn't changed by the electrical charge, so FM radio overcame and filtered out the noise. It didn't make any difference if thunderstorms were happening or not. It wasn't the amplitude that carried the intelligence; it was the frequency.

Listening to the Spirit

Your spirit man always hears from God, because God is living in your spirit. You are now in the process of learning how to filter out the spiritual or fleshly "noise" so you can hear more clearly from your spirit man.

I don't always hear what God is saying in my spirit the first time He says it, and neither do you. Don't tell me you do, because I know you're as human as I am! But God is gracious. He keeps repeating it until we get it. When we get quiet enough—when we get over in the Spirit realm—we pick up what He is saying.

For several years while I was still in the Air Force, I heard the word "ministry" in my spirit, and I was running around like a chicken with its head cut off trying to find more ways to be involved in the ministry. I found a lot of opportunities, and I was busy.

What God was really saying to me was, "Get into the ministry," but I wasn't hearing it straight, because I was in such a great mission field. I thought God wanted me to get involved in more ministry in the service. After all, there were more opportunities to minister to people who didn't know Jesus or didn't know anything about Him than anywhere I'd ever been.

I didn't understand at first that God wanted me to leave the service, but He did. He was telling me I was called to the ministry. He was showing me that I belonged in the ministry, and I had to leave the service to become a full-time minister of the Gospel.

Finally, I understood, and I did make the change, but it took me several years to get it straight. You may think, "You were pretty dull, weren't you?" Maybe I was, but God can help you, too.

The Inner Witness

I probably had more trouble hearing that particular direction than I would have had hearing others. God speaks by the inner witness. He ministers to us by that inner witness. It's a gentle, quiet witness. It's in your spirit, and you've got to be quiet to hear it correctly.

Sometimes you need to seek after what God is saying in order to receive it. If you seek it, you will find it. If you knock, it will be opened to you.

God is in the process of teaching you how to overcome the interference that is still in this world where the devil operates. People always ask, "Why did God put us in a place where He has confined the devil? That wasn't very nice!" It may not be nice in the way the world sees things, but it is necessary for you to overcome what the devil did.

As we studied earlier, the devil's kingdom includes the earth's atmosphere. His kingdom is centered in the earth, beneath the earth, and in the atmosphere around the earth.

According to Ephesians 3:10, God's manifold wisdom is being displayed to the whole universe—to all creation—by what He is doing today in the Church. God's plan for creation will be fulfilled the way He has ordained, in spite of all opposition.

"The Prince of Devils"

Another name the devil is called is "the prince of devils," found in Matthew 12:24. It speaks of his ability to rule over other spirit beings.

Actually, the kingdom of darkness is where he has his authority. The only authority he has is to operate in darkness. Darkness is his realm, and if you should join him in darkness, he can do a lot of harm to you.

However, believers are not in darkness. We have been translated. We have been delivered from the power and the authority of darkness.

You would have to take a deliberate step to disobey God and get in darkness. You ask, "Can it be done ignorantly?" Yes, you can do it ignorantly, but God can deal with ignorance a lot easier than He can with deliberate disobedience by Christians who are being enlightened by the Word of God. Deliberate disobedience is far worse than just ignorance.

In Matthew 12:22, we read where Jesus cast devils out of a man who was blind and dumb. The people were amazed to see the man speaking and seeing. They said of Jesus, "This is the Son of David!"

But when the Pharisees heard about it, they didn't say, "Hallelujah, this is the Messiah!" Instead, they said, "This fellow only casts out devils by Beelzebub, the prince of the devils" (v. 24).

That's what religion always says about true faith, so if someone calls you "Beelzebub," don't be dismayed. They called Jesus that, too. Religion still has that view.

Jesus knew their thoughts and said to them:

MATTHEW 12:25–26

25 Every kingdom divided against itself is brought to desolation; and every city or house divided against itself shall not stand.

26 And if Satan cast out Satan, he is divided against himself; how shall then his kingdom stand?

Beelzebub, the prince of the devils, is what we're looking at here. "The prince of demons" is what that means literally. The word is *daimon*, a word that means "demons," and it is translated "demons" in most translations of the Bible other than the *King James Version*. The *King James Version* never uses the word "demons." You won't find the word "demons" anywhere in the *King James Version*.

The translators of the *King James Version* translated this word *daimon* and another form of it, *daimonion*, as either "devils," "evil spirits," "fallen spirits," "unclean spirits," or something similar, but they never used the word "demons." Newer English translations use the word "demons" all the time, and they translate that word *daimon* as "demon."

Influenced by Fear

Satan is the prince of demons, devils, unclean spirits, and everything that is unclean or fallen in the kingdom of darkness. He is the ruler of darkness. He can have his way in darkness, but it isn't because all those fallen spirits love him. Demons don't have any loyalty! There is no love—nothing God-like—in the realm of darkness.

Satan inspires the fallen spirits by fear and force, because he is a more powerful spirit being than they are, and he can force them to do things. He can even influence people to do things through fear, if they listen to him.

He did that with the three nations that came to dispossess Israel. Second Chronicles 20 speaks of King Jehoshaphat. During his reign, three nations—Moab, Ammon, and Mount Seir (Edom)—who were actually cousins of the Jews—conspired and joined forces to kick the Jews out of the land of Israel.

King Jehoshaphat turned to God. The word of God came to a Levite named Jahaziel, and he prophesied, *"Ye shall not need to fight in this battle...stand ye still, and see the salvation* [or deliverance] *of the Lord with you"* (2 Chron. 20:17).

God instructed them to go out the next day and sing hymns and praises to Him. They did. As they marched toward the place God told them their enemies would be, they sang, "Praise the Lord, for His mercy endures forever." They sang that simple chorus for three hours!

When Your Spirit Rejoices

Sometimes we get nervous if we have to sing the same chorus for five minutes! If you've ever led choruses, you know people get nervous when you sing the same words too long. But sometimes God wants you to sing those words over and over again.

You say, "That's boring." No, it's not boring. That's what your flesh thinks, but your spirit man rejoices to have the Word implanted in it like that.

If you were to measure how far the cliff of Ziz is from Jerusalem, you would find it takes about three hours to walk there. When the Jews walked that distance, singing obediently to God, He set ambushments against their enemies. That doesn't mean He ambushed the Ammonites, the Moabites, or the Edomites. He didn't do anything to *them.*

What enemies did He ambush? *Spirit beings!* Who got the Ammonites, Moabites, and Edomites to agree to this common purpose to dispossess Israel? Spirit beings! As soon as God ambushed those spirit beings, they disappeared. God's angels drove them away as God's covenant people praised Him!

While the three armies were marching along to dispossess Israel, the Ammonites and Moabites looked at the fellows from Edom/Mt. Seir and said, "Why are we marching with them? We hate their guts! While we've got them out here in the wilderness, why don't we take advantage of the situation and kill them?" Swords in hand, they attacked them.

While they were doing that, they looked at each other and said, "Come to think of it, I don't like you any better than I do them"—and the remaining armies attacked each other! When they were done, no one was left alive.

Genuine Unity

They didn't have any genuine unity of purpose, because they didn't have any love or genuine regard for each other. They were pushed into acting together, but when the evil spirits that were influencing them were no longer around, the three nations followed the inclinations of their flesh and killed each other!

We believers have a great advantage. Thank God, we can have real unity of the Spirit. We are of one Spirit, one Lord, one faith, and one baptism, the Bible says, and we can choose to walk in the light of that unity.

In darkness, there is no unity at all. If the devil is not around, the demons do their own thing. You can inspire people with fear, but if you're not there to keep inspiring them with fear, they won't obey.

It's like the old saying, "When the cat's away, the mice will play." The mice are afraid of the cat. When the cat's not there, the mice do whatever they please.

In the service, some people tried to lead us through fear. They thought that was the best way to rule. They thought if they were bigger and badder than anyone else and made us afraid of them, we would do what they told us to do. But when they weren't there, their efforts failed utterly, because people weren't loyal to them.

Limitations of Satan's Kingdom

That's the way it is in the kingdom of darkness. Fallen spirits are not loyal to the devil. They don't love the devil. They only do his bidding because they are afraid of him. When he is not present with them, they do whatever they feel like doing. Therefore, the devil doesn't rule over some monolithic realm where everything is in perfect order. It's nothing like that. It's a real mess!

I'm not trying to have a pity party for the devil. Don't feel sorry for him. His fall was his own fault, and every fallen being that is with him is there because they chose to live in darkness. Fallen beings have no love, no faith—nothing like that—and they have no hope, either, because it is hopeless in the kingdom of darkness. In contrast, believers live blessed lives.

When I was unsaved, I didn't realize all of that. I didn't understand what darkness had done to me. I got saved in 1964, but I can't tell you today what it was like to be unsaved. I do remember I didn't have much joy, peace, happiness, or anything like that, but I don't remember all the details.

Jesus has been living in me so long, I don't know what it's like to be without Him. Sometimes we take His presence for granted, and we go about our business.

However, if the Spirit of God were withdrawn from us for even an instant, it would be a horror of darkness to us, because we've been formed in the likeness of Christ.

Although Satan has authority to operate in darkness, he does not have authority in your life. The Word of God took it away from him and gave it back to you. Don't give him a place!

"The God of This World"

Satan's next title is found in Second Corinthians 4:4, where he is called "the god of this world." Do you see how names like this reveal his position and also some of his activities?

Verse 3 says, *"If our gospel be hid, it is hid to them that are lost."* Who do you suppose it is that hides it from those who are lost? Satan does. Even if they do hear the Gospel, he comes and tries to steal it immediately, before it can work in their lives. Some people allow him to steal it.

Verse 4 continues, *"The god of this world [Satan] hath blinded the minds of them which believe not, lest the light of the glorious gospel of Christ, who is the image of God, should shine unto them."*

The minds of unbelievers are what? *Blinded.* Who blinds them? *The devil.* What are they blind to? *The truth.* They think they know the truth, and they think they are pursuing it, but they don't know the truth, because the god of this world has blinded their minds. And until their minds are disconnected from that dead spirit they've got, they are going to remain that way! When a person gets saved, the process of the renewal of his or her mind begins.

Although Satan is called "the god of this world," it doesn't mean he *owns* the world. The world is the Lord's and the fullness thereof. However, Satan has been granted a time during which he can operate in this world. While he is still here, he is called "the god of this world."

The word "world" here is not *kosmos*, like it was in his title "the prince of this world." Instead, it is the Greek word *aion*, which means "age." That limits how long Satan is going to be here.

Satan's "Retirement Plan"

In the Book of Revelation, you find a day when an angel comes down from Heaven holding a key to the bottomless pit and a chain. He opens the pit, binds the devil with the chain, and casts him into it. That's Satan's "retirement plan" being executed! It marks the end of the time he may freely operate in this world. After that, he is allowed to operate for only a brief time.

You are not going to have to deal with him in eternity. He will have been dealt with completely by then. As far as you are concerned, you will never even think about him again, which will be good. There won't be any remembrance in Heaven of what he did on earth and how he created misery for human beings.

Satan is the god of this age, literally, and this age has an ending. We learn from the Word that Satan's present position in this world, the *kosmos*, comes to an end at the end of the age. The *New American Standard Bible* and other translations say that he is "the god of this age."

In Revelation chapter 9, we find other names that give Satan the ability to operate in this world. They also refer to the bottomless pit that will be opened in the time of great tribulation. With the next names, we begin to look at those which primarily show his activity.

Who Is in the Bottomless Pit?

Do you know what is in the bottomless pit? *Fallen angels.* Do you know what will come out of it when it's opened? Fallen angels. Some writers have said it contains helicopters, guns, bombs, or napalm, but there is nothing like that in the bottomless pit. When it is opened, fallen angels will come out, because that is where most of them were imprisoned.

When they come out, they will have power to afflict the ungodly. They will torment those who do not have the seal of God in their foreheads. Men and women will have what they say, whether they call on good or evil. The more they call on evil, the more evil works will be manifested, because of their evil words. People truly do have what they say, good or bad.

There will be some, even in the time of great tribulation, who have believed God—but there will be a great many more who haven't, and they will be the ones who will be tormented when the bottomless pit is opened. Their tormenters will make this the worst time people on earth have ever known!

Revelation 9:11 tells us these beings *"had a king over them, which is the angel of the bottomless pit, whose name in the Hebrew tongue is Abaddon, but in the Greek tongue hath his name Apollyon."* Both names mean the same thing: "destroyer." Who is the destroyer? Satan. What does he come to do? Steal, kill, and *destroy!*

Jesus, speaking of the great tribulation, noted, *"And except those days should be shortened, there should no flesh be saved: but for the elect's sake those days shall be shortened"* (Matt. 24:22). That's how bad it's going to be. I'm glad I'm not going to be walking around in the natural on earth in that day!

The Tempter

However, God told all believers we would suffer tribulation. In First Thessalonians 3:4, we read, *"For verily, when we were with you, we told you before that we should suffer tribulation."*

Who sees to it that you have tribulation? Satan. *God doesn't send tribulation.* He doesn't dole it out to you. God is not involved in it.

Although God has put you in a world where He knew you would have tribulation, He has also given you everything you need to overcome it.

Verse 5 continues, *"when I could no longer forbear, I sent to know your faith, lest by some means the tempter have tempted you, and our labour be in vain."* This means that Paul sent someone back to Thessalonica to find out whether the believers there were remaining firm in the faith or not.

The Parable of the Sower

Do you remember the Parable of the Sower? Often when we read that parable, we think, "There are some people who are like the place where the seed fell on stony ground, and there are some people who are like the place where the seed fell by the wayside.

"There are also some who are like the place where weeds, thistles, and thorns choke out the Word—and, finally, there are some people who are good ground."

Believe and confess that you are the *good* ground. You can recall in your own life times when you heard the Word and it was immediately stolen away.

You thought, "That's not right," because man-made traditions didn't agree with what you heard. There were times when you heard the Word, but you didn't do what you should have done with it. There were other times when you let the cares of this world come in and choke the Word. But thank God for the times when you've been good ground!

A Good Report

That is why Paul sent someone to find out what kind of ground the believers in Thessalonica turned out to be. He also wanted to know what kind of help they needed. The messenger returned and gave Paul a good report. The believers in Thessalonica had overcome a lot of tribulation and many attempts to steal their faith.

Paul was pleased when he heard that report, and he commended them for it. There is much commendation in this epistle. However, Paul was concerned that the tempter—that's Satan—had tempted them in some way, and the faith he had instilled in them had somehow been stolen.

Jesus Himself was tempted, tested, and tried in every way we are, yet He remained without sin. Jesus was never overcome by temptation; He always overcame it.

Jesus' three greatest temptations are mentioned in Matthew chapter 4. Satan tempted Him in the wilderness, yet angels of God came and ministered to Him in the wilderness.

We have the same comfort and help Jesus had. If He needed help, guess who else needs help? We do!

7

How to Deal With the Devil

If you yield to Satan after you have heard the Word of God, he can steal it away from you before you apply it to your life. He uses different means to do that, including your background.

Some of you came from backgrounds where you heard the teaching that speaking in tongues is of the devil. Thus, when someone started to share something from the Word with you about speaking in tongues, your first thought was, "Oh, no, that's of the devil!" Why? Because you'd heard that opinion from people you respected; from people who had told you the truth about other things.

Traditional thinking is the hardest thing to overcome—worse even than unbelief. Unbelief is easy to overcome, because all you've got to do is hear what the Word says and act on it. That overcomes unbelief.

To overcome traditional thinking, either from the Church or from the world around you, requires renewing the mind, and that takes time. It's a process.

Why Tests Come

After Jesus was baptized in the Jordan River, He went into the wilderness, where He was tested. Testing comes because you have been blessed. It comes because the enemy knows God has invested something in you, and he is trying to steal it before you ever get to apply it.

If he can't steal it that way, he'll try to take your attention away from the Word at a time when you need to give your full attention to it. There are many different ways he does that.

Jesus overcame all of Satan's temptations. Matthew 4:1–3 says:

MATTHEW 4:1–3

1 Then was Jesus led up of the spirit into the wilderness to be tempted of the devil.

2 And when he had fasted forty days and forty nights, he was afterward an hungered.

3 And when the tempter came to him, he said, If thou be the Son of God....

How unwise the devil is! There he was, trying to tempt Jesus! He knew that Jesus had become human, so he thought he could work his wiles on Jesus' humanity. But Jesus never allowed him to do it.

The devil says the same kind of thing to you: "If you were *really* called, wouldn't all kinds of provision be waiting for you when you get there?" That makes you think, "Why do I have to go through a test to get it?" Because it is common to man; that's why. If you didn't know any more than that, it would be enough.

"But So-and-so got it without any test," you complain. It may seem like that to you, but it doesn't mean that person got what he sought without any test.

Tested, Tempted, and Tried

Peter said, *"Beloved, think it not strange concerning the fiery trial that is to try* [test or tempt] *you"* (1 Peter 4:12). It is common to everyone's experience. It happens to all of us, because we are living in this world and we are human beings.

Jesus, Who had been made man for our salvation, was tested, tempted, and tried in all points like we are, the Word of God says in Hebrews 4:15. How He responded to it is what we need to study here.

In the wilderness, Satan challenged Him, *"If thou be the Son of God, command that these stones be made bread. But he answered and said, It is written"* (Matt. 4:3–4). That's a good way to answer the devil, isn't it? *The Word of God is always our answer.*

The account continues:

MATTHEW 4:4–6

4 It is written, Man shall not live by bread alone, but by every word that proceedeth out of the mouth of God.

5 Then the devil taketh him up into the holy city, and setteth him on a pinnacle of the temple,

6 And saith unto him, If thou be the Son of God, cast thyself down: for it is written.

Misquoting Scripture

Next, the devil quoted from the 91st Psalm: *"He shall give his angels charge concerning thee: and in their hands they shall bear thee up, lest at any time thou dash thy foot against a stone"* (Matt. 4:6).

Some point out that the devil didn't quote this verse exactly. That's not the point. How do you know it was translated perfectly? Many things Jesus said aren't the same words as recorded in your Old Testament. Often when He was quoting a scripture, it wasn't quoted word for word the way you read it in your Old Testament, so you don't really know whether He quoted it perfectly or not.

Whether Jesus said "an" instead of "the" or something is not the point. The point is, *Satan always misapplies scripture when he quotes it.* A misapplication of scripture is a lie. Satan is a liar, even when quoting scripture!

God never tells us to put His Word to the test in a foolish way, like jumping off the pinnacle of the Temple. The lie is that Satan was telling Jesus to do something with Matthew 4:6 that God never intended.

Protect Yourself With Scripture

How can you avoid such a temptation? By knowing what else the Word of God says. In the same temptation, you will see how Jesus answered the devil with more of God's Word.

Satan quoted what the 91st Psalm says, but Jesus also knew what else the Word says. He wasn't a one-verse man. He didn't have His favorite verses and hang everything He knew on them.

Thank God, we are familiar with Mark 11:23–24, and we need to be—but we also need to be familiar with the *whole* counsel of God (Acts 20:27). Jesus escaped misapplying the Word of God because He knew the rest of the counsel of God.

What does that teach you? You need to stay in contact with the larger context, not just your favorite verses or books. The *whole* counsel of God reveals things that impact on any verse.

There are different contexts. There is the immediate context in which the verse is found. There is the context of that whole chapter. There is the context of that book in the Bible. There is the context of which Testament the verse is found in. And there is also the context of the whole Bible. All of that tells you something about how to interpret the Word.

What Else the Word Says

You need to stay in contact with the whole context, because that is how Jesus escaped misapplying the Word. He knew what *else* the Word said. If you know what else it says, and you know how to apply it and interpret it, you won't be deceived!

I like plans where you devote 15 minutes a day to reading the Bible, and at the end of the year, you'll have read through the whole Bible. Such plans keep you in regular contact with the whole counsel of God.

In Kenneth E. Hagin's 1985 Campmeeting in Tulsa, Mrs. Gordon Lindsay from Christ For the Nations in Dallas, told the gathering that she felt really blessed that year because she had just finished reading the Bible through for the forty-second time.

When we heard Mrs. Lindsay say that, my wife, June, and I resolved to start reading through the Bible each year, and we have done so ever since, a little each day. It has been a great blessing to us.

Jesus Outwits the Devil

Jesus recognized the devil's devices and said:

MATTHEW 4:7–10

7 It is written again, Thou shalt not tempt the Lord thy God.

8 Again, the devil taketh him up into an exceeding high mountain, and sheweth him all the kingdoms of the world, and the glory of them;

9 And saith unto Him, All these things will I give thee, if thou wilt fall down and worship me.

10 Then saith Jesus unto him, Get thee hence, Satan: for it is written, Thou shalt worship the Lord thy God, and him only shalt thou serve.

Jesus came to bring the truth to all the kingdoms of the world. The devil, however, wants you to think there's a shortcut—some easy way you can take to get your job done—something that doesn't take any dedication, commitment, or work. He'll say, "Here it is, all handed to you—simple." But it's not that simple.

Jesus said, *"Go ye into all the world, and preach the gospel to every creature"* (Mark 16:15)—but He didn't say the devil would deliver the whole world to you.

Do you think if Jesus had bowed down and worshipped the devil, he really would have given Him all those kingdoms? No, he wouldn't. He promises all kinds of things he won't do. Remember, he's a liar. He's *always* a liar.

There is no easy way to accomplish what God has given you to do for the rest of your life. Something that is going to take your whole life to complete isn't going to be done in a day, a week, or even a year. So don't look for quick solutions or easy ways, which was what the devil was trying to do with Jesus.

Jesus responded, *"Get thee hence, Satan: for it is written, Thou shalt worship the Lord thy God, and him only shalt thou serve"* (Matt. 4:10). The next verse tells us, *"Then the devil leaveth him, and, behold, angels came and ministered unto him"* (v. 11).

"The Accuser of the Brethren"

The next name Satan is called is "the accuser of the brethren" in Revelation 12:10, where the apostle John said:

REVELATION 12:10

10 I heard a loud voice saying in heaven, Now is come salvation, and strength, and the kingdom of our God, and the power of his Christ: for the accuser of our brethren is cast down, which accused them before our God day and night.

The kingdom of God has come! Where is the kingdom today? Praise the Lord, it's living in us.

The accuser's fall isn't something that is going to happen in the future. It happened when the devil drew the third part of the stars of heaven down with him.

Satan can no longer accuse you before God in Heaven. He can go around mouthing all he wants to, but it doesn't have to affect you. All you need to do is tell him to shut up in Jesus' Name, and that will be the end of that.

"What About Job?"

"What about Job?" someone will ask. "Didn't the devil go up to Heaven and accuse Job?"

No, he did not. The Bible doesn't say he did. It says Satan *accused* Job before God. You can do that without going up to Heaven.

Job 1:6–11 says:

JOB 1:6–11

6 Now there was a day when the sons of God [in this case, His angels] came to present themselves before the Lord, and Satan came also among them.

7 And the Lord said unto Satan, Whence comest thou? Then Satan answered the Lord, and said, From going to and fro in the earth, and from walking up and down in it.

8 And the Lord said unto Satan, Hast thou considered my servant Job, that there is none like him in the earth, a perfect and an upright man, one that fears God, and escheweth [avoids] evil?

9 Then Satan answered the Lord, and said, Doth Job fear God for nought?

10 Hast not thou made an hedge about him, and about his house, and about all that he hath on every side? thou hast blessed the work of his hands, and his substance is increased in the land.

11 But put forth thine hand now, and touch all that he hath, and he will curse thee to thy face.

So Satan went out to begin his efforts against Job. Notice there is no mention of Heaven in that passage. Do you see the word "Heaven" anywhere? People assume that because Satan accused Job before God, he did so in Heaven, but the Bible doesn't say so.

A Time of Restoration

In Zechariah chapter 3, we find a similar situation, and from it we can draw insights into what happened in Job's life. This chapter describes a time of restoration in Jerusalem, a time when God was fulfilling the promises He had made in His Word to restore the Jews to their homeland after being carried off into captivity.

During the 70 years of the captivity, there had been no high priest officiating in the Temple in Jerusalem, because Nebuchadnezzar had destroyed that Temple. It needed to be rebuilt, and when it was about to be finished, the high priest had charge of what went on in that Temple.

Without a high priest to make atonement for them every year, the Jews had suffered. Now the people of Israel had returned from captivity to reinstate worship in their Temple.

Whenever a new high priest appeared on the scene, can you imagine how the devil attacked him? "What makes you think you can go into the Holy of Holies? What makes you think the ceremony will do any good?"

The Ark of the Covenant never reappeared after that captivity. No one knows where it went or what happened to it. Movie makers may think they do, but they don't. It's not waiting to be dug up someplace. God isn't living in that ark underground in some hole where someone buried it. Even though there was no ark, the service of that Temple would be restored by faith in God's Word.

Satan Resists the High Priest

Joshua was chosen from among the Levites to become the new high priest. This man was not the same Joshua who lived in the days of Moses; this was a priest named Joshua.

Zechariah 3:1 says, *"He showed me Joshua the high priest standing before the angel of the Lord, and Satan standing at his right hand to resist him."*

In the Old Testament, when God came to this earth and appeared to men, He most often appeared in the form of "the angel of the Lord," looking like a man or an angel, the messenger of the Lord and His covenant.

Joshua the high priest was standing before the angel of the Lord, and Satan was standing at his right hand to resist him. All of this happened here on the earth.

ZECHARIAH 3:2–3

2 And the Lord said unto Satan, The Lord rebuke thee, O Satan; even the Lord that hath chosen Jerusalem rebuke thee: is not this [the priest Joshua] a brand plucked out of the fire?

3 Now Joshua was clothed with filthy garments, and stood before the angel.

Joshua's own righteousness would not be enough for him to do the work of the high priest.

ZECHARIAH 3:4

4 And he answered and spake unto those that stood before him [the other angelic beings], saying, Take away the filthy garments from him.

We know it was God Himself appearing in the earth because of what He just said. Is there any angel He created that would say, "I have caused your iniquity to pass from you?" No, no angel would say that. Only a false angel sent by the devil would say something like that. Only God can make iniquity pass away from man or can forgive a man's sins.

Verse 4 continues, *"Behold, I have caused thine iniquity to pass from thee, and I will clothe thee with change of raiment."*

In other words, God said, "I will give you rightstanding to do the work of the high priest and to bless you personally."

ZECHARIAH 3:5–7

5 And I said, Let them set a fair mitre [a headpiece symbolizing a measure of anointing given to him] upon his head. So they set a fair mitre upon his head, and clothed him with garments. And the angel of the Lord stood by.

6 And the angel of the Lord protested unto Joshua, saying,

7 Thus saith the Lord of hosts; If thou wilt walk in my ways, and if thou wilt keep my charge, then thou shalt also judge my house, and shalt also keep my courts, and I will give thee places to walk among these that stand by [in the angelic company].

Satan wasn't the only one there, but he was there. And where did all this happen? On earth. It doesn't say one word about Heaven. The angel of the Lord appeared on the earth, and Satan appeared before him. He accuses us before God, but not in Heaven, because where is God now? He's in you! So when Satan comes and accuses you, he's accusing you before God.

It's not like Satan has to travel up to Heaven and stand before the throne of God, with Jesus seated at His right hand, and open his mouth to accuse you.

Do you think the God of the whole universe is going to let Satan go up to Heaven and blaspheme, lie, and accuse? Of course not! It doesn't square with what else we know about Heaven. You shouldn't let him do it to you, either.

Don't Accuse the Brethren

God doesn't coexist with evil. However, there is evil in this world, and you need to overcome it. Satan is the accuser of the brethren. Why should you help him by accusing someone else? Why would you want to share in his work?

"But I want to get even with someone!"

No, you don't.

"He owes me 50 cents."

Forgive him.

"He owes me more than that."

"Forgive that, too."

Romans 2:1–3 is written to believers:

ROMANS 2:1-3
1 Therefore thou art inexcusable, O man, whosoever thou art that judgest [devalues or judges as worthless]: for wherein thou judgest another, thou condemnest thyself; for thou that judgest doest the same things.
2 But we are sure that the judgment of God is according to truth against them which commit such things
3 And thinkest thou this, O man, that judgest them which do such things, and doest the same, that thou shalt escape the judgment of God?

If you are not going to escape the thing you are accusing someone else of, why would you want to accuse them of it? It's going to end up back on you. You shouldn't go around accusing others. That's the work of the devil. He's the accuser of the brethren.

The Importance of Restoration

"But what if these people *need* to be disciplined?"

Follow the scriptural ways of doing it. What is the scriptural purpose of disciplining someone? To *restore* him, not to kick him out, defame him, or make him appear worthless!

Romans 8:1 says, *"There is therefore now no condemnation to them which are in Christ Jesus."* If you know that, why would you want to condemn a person for having done wrong? There is no condemnation to those who are in Christ Jesus.

If you know a believer has done wrong, should you want to condemn him? No, you should want to restore such a person in the spirit of meekness, Paul instructs in Galatians 6:1, considering yourself, lest *you* also be tempted.

"For the law of the Spirit of life in Christ Jesus hath made me free from the law of sin and death" (Rom. 8:2). If a believer is free, why would you want to reengage him in condemnation? If the will of God is to free him from condemnation, why would you want to be involved in putting it back on him? That's the devil's work.

We have an Advocate if we've done wrong, and that Advocate is Jesus Christ, the Righteous One. He shows us exactly what to do if we have done wrong. And if we do this, the Bible says He has forgiven us and cleansed us from all unrighteousness.

While I was serving in the military, I heard that the only army that shoots its wounded is the army of the Lord—the Church. We shouldn't have such a reputation. We shouldn't be shooting our wounded or holding them up for public scorn and ridicule. We should be covering what they did.

Love covers what? A multitude of sins, according to First Peter 4:8. If you love people, you'll *cover* their transgressions; you won't *expose* them.

"The Deceiver"

The next name Satan is called in the Word of God is "deceiver." Second Corinthians 11:13 says this about him: *"For such are false apostles, deceitful workers, transforming themselves into the apostles of Christ."*

Paul was concerned about false apostles who were infecting the Corinthian church. He called them deceitful workers. They were human beings, but they transformed themselves into "the apostles of Christ."

Can you really do that? Can you make yourself an apostle of Christ? No, but you can make it *look* like you are. It doesn't mean you *are* one.

That's the whole point with this area of deception. The devil does many things to make him look like something he isn't. He deceives, masquerades, and disguises himself.

Paul writes in verse 14, *"And no marvel; for Satan himself is transformed into an angel of light."* He can make himself appear to a human being as an angel of light. However, if you are seeing him by the light of the Holy Spirit and the light of the Word of God, you would never see him that way.

He has no light in him—no light whatsoever. Only to the senses of a human being can he disguise himself and appear as an angel of light. He's darkness, and he can't return to what he was. He has been cast out of the kingdom of light by God's Word. This is an important point. Many people misunderstand it.

Deceived by a Bright Light

I once had a Bible school student from another nation who thought the Lord was going to return that October. She was convinced, because a bright light had appeared in her church while they were praying and told them the Lord was coming on such-and-such a date.

Of course, Jesus didn't come on that date. That was a lie. What did the light appear to? Their senses. It wasn't from the heart. It wasn't in agreement with the Word of God; in fact, it was totally contrary to the Word of God.

You can see all the bright lights there are and still not see God. *Something supernatural doesn't mean it's from God.* There are a lot of supernatural things that aren't from God.

How can you know the difference? That which is from God always agrees with the Word of God, and that which is not from God will disagree with the Word of God in some way.

"Therefore it is no great thing if his ministers [those who follow Satan in his ministry] *also be transformed as the ministers of righteousness; whose end shall be according to their works"* (v. 15). These persons appear to be ministers of righteousness.

Masquerading Ministers

I was reared in a denominational church. Few if any of the pastors in our church were saved, but they all claimed to be ministers of God. They didn't tell us the truth. They told us lies.

They preached out of *Reader's Digest!* They hardly ever opened the Bible. If they did, they read a little and promptly closed it again. They all wore their collars backwards, though. They looked very religious, but they were not godly.

It's a masquerade when you go around in black clothing and a white collar and look godly according to the world but not according to God. God didn't tell these people to dress like that. You don't become something because you dress a certain way. However, if ministers are saved and want to dress that way, let them; I don't care.

Masquerades make someone else think you're something you're not. Many people masquerade while wearing regular clothing, too. The Bible calls them "grievous wolves" (Acts 20:29).

Think Soberly

Part of being a deceiver and appearing as an angel of light is covered by Peter in First Peter 5:8, where he says, *"Be sober."* This doesn't mean to quit drinking; you're supposed to have already done that. It refers to how you think. Think how? Think soberly.

In other words, don't accept everything you hear. Think about things first. Is that new idea or doctrine you're thinking of embracing godly or not? If you judge things by what you know of God's Word, you'll be a much less likely candidate for deception.

Peter advises, *"Be sober, be vigilant, because your adversary the devil, as a roaring lion, walketh about, seeking whom he may devour"* (v. 8).

The devil tries to make you believe he's a roaring lion. However, you have dominion over the animal kingdom! You should be concerned about the situation, but you don't need to be afraid of the devil. You just need to do something about him.

So if the devil shows up, don't think you can ignore him, and he'll go away. That isn't going to work. You're going to have to take your dominion and deal with him scripturally, just like Jesus did. He told Satan, "It is written, Satan."

Like a Roaring Lion

The devil will come around *like* a roaring lion, trying to impress you that he has an ability he does not have. When he appears before a Spirit-filled, Word-oriented believer and roars, he usually gets his comeuppance quickly.

Do you remember seeing the MGM lion roar at the beginning of old movies? When the lion roars, he's really impressive. Another film company, just as a joke, has a little kitten that goes, "Meow." That's more like what the devil is really like. He isn't anything like the lion, because the lion has teeth, and all of Satan's were pulled by Jesus Christ!

The devil walks around as a roaring lion. He wants to instill fear in you. Did you know you can *feel* afraid but not *be* afraid? Fear can grip your flesh and make you feel afraid, but the man on the inside—full of the Word of God and filled with the Holy Spirit—stands up against fear. Then Satan *must* flee from you.

His bluffing techniques are part of his being a deceiver. He walks about, but he's not omnipresent. He can only be in one place at a time. He walks about as a roaring lion, seeking whom he may devour. If someone gives him access by his fearful act, he will devour them. However, if you don't give him access, he can't devour you.

Again and again in the Word of God you see the admonition not to be afraid. There is nothing to be afraid of, because you are in God, and He is in you!

The King of the Beasts

A story is told about the lion, the king of the beasts. The lion was walking around in the jungle one day, feeling proud of himself and his station in life.

As he was strolling around, he saw a zebra grazing, and he roared at him, "Grrr—who's the king of the beasts?"

The zebra looked at him and thought, "I can run faster than he can, but I'm enjoying my lunch, and I want to keep on enjoying it." He said, *"You* are, O mighty lion."

The lion got even more puffed up, and he walked a little farther through the jungle. The next animal he encountered was a giraffe that was nibbling his lunch from the top of a tall tree. The tender leaves up there were quite tasty, and he didn't want to be disturbed, either.

When the lion roared at him, "Grrr—who's the king of the beasts?" he replied, *"You* are, mighty lion," and kept eating his lunch.

By now the lion was really puffed up, so he went down to the river. When he got there, he saw an elephant getting a drink of water. He roared at him, "Grrr—who's the king of the beasts?"

The elephant looked at him, grabbed him in his trunk, and flung him clear across the river, where he landed in the mud.

Dazed, the lion popped his head out of the mud, looked back at the elephant, and said, "You don't have to get mad just because you don't know the answer!"

Act Like the Elephant

Act like that elephant, because you *are* like the elephant. When the devil comes around roaring at you, make him wish he had never showed up. Stir up what's in you, and speak the Word of God that's in your heart. He'll flee from you. He is terrorized by that.

No weapon he can form against you will prosper. When you speak the Word of God from a believing heart, he will run.

Satan is not the king of your domain; *you are the king in your domain.* Jesus is king over the whole kingdom of Heaven, and you are a prince or princess in it.

Take your authority. Take your dominion. Don't let the devil come around, roar at you, and cause you to give up your inheritance. His act is a deception!

The elephant knew who the real king is. So did the zebra and the giraffe. They didn't worry about the lion. They weren't impressed because he *thought* he was the king of the beasts. Neither should we be impressed because the devil thinks he can trick us. We know better. We're not ignorant of his devices.

How To Approach the Enemy

Another name Satan is called in verse 8 is "adversary," a word that means "enemy." The devil is opposing you. He is contrary to everything you are. That's why he acts the way he does.

Some bulls are very cantankerous, either by their nature or their training. If you go into their field and wave a red flag at them, they'll charge that flag. Some of them are so mean, if you walk into their territory, red flag or not, they will charge you.

What if you drove into their field in a red truck? They would charge, but they would wish they hadn't when they hit the truck!

That's the way you approach the enemy—wearing the whole armor of God. He is the one at the disadvantage when you are walking in the Spirit. You have no disadvantage whatsoever.

However, the devil is an adversary. He is diligent about it. He is opposed to you, and he isn't going to change just because you don't like it. That's the way he is going to act from now until the end of the age.

You can't change that. You can't change what he attempts to do to you as your adversary—but you can change the outcome of such encounters every time!

8

Overcoming the Adversary

First Peter 5:8 states that the devil, your adversary, walks about as a roaring lion, seeking whom he may devour. The word that is translated "adversary" is also translated "enemy" in Matthew 13.

If someone is "adverse" to you, it means he is opposed to you. He is the opposite of what you are. Satan is also opposite to and opposed to God. He is opposed to everything God is and does. Therefore, when you live, move, and have your being in Christ, Satan is opposed to you.

If opposition comes to you while you're living the Christian life, what does that indicate? It means you are living a Christian life!

Persecution won't come to you if you're not living the Christian life. You'll still get in trouble, but it will be of your own doing, through the works of your flesh. The devil doesn't need to do anything about that. If you walk contrary to God's Word, you will eat the fruit of your own way, and that's not pleasant.

But if you walk the way Jesus walked, you will have opposition, because you have an adversary. This is not a "gloom-and-doom" message; it's simply a fact.

Jesus said, *"In the world ye shall have tribulation: but be of good cheer; I have overcome the world"* (John 16:33). You are to be of good cheer because you are in Him, overcoming the world. This is the victory that overcomes the world, the faith God has given to believers.

Having opposition doesn't prove you missed it, although many people think it does. When they run into opposition, they immediately think, "I must have done something wrong." No, they did something right. That's why they're having opposition.

So don't count opposition as something terrible. Peter said, *"Beloved, think it not strange concerning the fiery trial which is to try you, as though some strange thing happened unto you"* (1 Peter 4:12). It's not strange—it's normal—because you're living in Christ.

Trials happen to every believer, so it's not unusual for you to experience them—and the more you walk in obedience, the more trials you will have.

Paul's Many Trials

Look at the apostle Paul. In Second Corinthians chapter 11, Paul shares a long list of things he suffered during his missionary journeys.

2 CORINTHIANS 11:23–28

23 Are they ministers of Christ?...I am more; in labours more abundant, in stripes above measure, in prisons more frequent, in deaths oft.

24 Of the Jews five times received I forty stripes save one.

25 Thrice was I beaten with rods, once was I stoned, thrice I suffered shipwreck, a night and a day I have been in the deep;

26 In journeyings often, in perils of waters, in perils of robbers, in perils by mine own countrymen, in perils by the heathen, in perils in the city, in perils in the wilderness, in perils in the sea, in perils among false brethren;

27 In weariness and painfulness, in watchings often, in hunger and thirst, in fastings often, in cold and nakedness.

28 Beside those things that are without, that which cometh upon me daily, the care of all the churches.

The wrong time to stop believing is when you're in a test or trial. Remember, you have an adversary. He's the one that's putting the pressure on you, but God will deliver you out of it—always, always, always. Paul was persecuted beyond measure, yet he said the Lord had delivered him out of all his difficulties (2 Tim. 3:11).

Accept the fact that Satan is going to work against you. You can't change that fact, but you can keep him from preventing you from doing what God told you to do. That's exactly what Paul did.

Overcoming took time, but Paul was never thwarted or stopped by what the enemy did.

Paul Didn't Avoid Persecution

Think about this: Every time Paul went to a new city, he went first to the synagogue. A few Jews in those synagogues may have believed in Jesus Christ as the Messiah, but most didn't. A fallen spirit sent by the adversary stirred up the religious people, and they opposed and persecuted Paul.

You'd think that after five or six experiences like that, Paul would say to himself, "If I don't go to the synagogue in the next town, I'll have a much easier time. I'll leave them alone." But that's not the way Paul acted.

The Jews were on Paul's heart. His heart's desire was to see them believe in Christ. He said he'd lay his life down if only it would help them believe (Rom. 9:3)—and he meant it!

Paul never stopped going to his fellow Jews, even though every time he did, it resulted in great persecution for him. Even when Paul was stoned, and was dragged out of the city and left for dead, he recovered, got up, returned to the city, and departed the next day for another city.

You don't even get up and go back into the city the day you've been stoned without a miracle. You don't go anywhere the day after you've been stoned unless there has been a notable miracle. But Paul had a notable miracle that delivered him from all the intentions of the adversary.

Tares and Wheat

In Matthew chapter 13, Jesus was speaking in parables. Verses 24–28 relate:

MATTHEW 13:24–28

24 Another parable put he forth unto them, saying, The kingdom of heaven is likened unto a man which sowed good seed in his field:

25 But while men slept, his enemy came and sowed tares among the wheat, and went his way.

26 But when the blade was sprung up, and brought forth fruit, then appeared the tares also.

27 So the servants of the householder came and said unto him, Sir, didst not thou sow good seed in thy field? from whence then hath it tares?

28 He said unto them, An enemy hath done this.

"Enemy" is the same word that is translated "adversary" in First Peter 5:8. Satan is an enemy, an adversary, to you.

MATTHEW 13:28–30

28 The servants said unto him, Wilt thou then that we go and gather them up?

29 But he said, Nay; lest while ye gather up the tares, ye root up also the wheat with them.

30 Let both grow together until the harvest: and in the time of harvest I will say to the reapers, Gather ye together first the tares, and bind them in bundles to burn them: but gather the wheat into my barn.

After teaching some other things, Jesus sent the multitude away, and when He was alone with His disciples, they asked Him, *"Declare unto us the parable of the tares of the field"* (v. 36).

Jesus Answers

Jesus always explained things to the disciples when they asked Him to. He never said, "No, I can't do that for you." If you ask Him to explain something that you don't understand in the Word of God, He will explain it to you. Instead of asking people, you ought to ask Him.

MATTHEW 13:37–38

37 He answered and said unto them, He that soweth the good seed is the Son of man [the Word of God].

38 The field is the world; the good seed are the children of the kingdom; but the tares are the children of the wicked one.

In other words, the whole world is to be seeded with the Word of God. The good seed are all those whose names are written in the Lamb's Book of Life. "The wicked one" is another name for Satan. *"The children of the wicked one"* are the tares in this parable. But the good news is: Tares can become wheat!

Through the new birth, a child of the devil can become a child of God. That's what Jesus was really teaching about. He was discussing what happens when there is a new birth. When someone is regenerated, that child of the devil becomes a child of God.

I'm certainly glad God didn't weed out all of the tares before I became wheat, because I used to be a tare. Thank God, tares can be changed into wheat! But only God can do such a thing.

You can't do it yourself in the natural. That's why Jesus said, "Don't rip the tares out." He knew many of them were going to become wheat. Who is it we're to preach the gospel to: wheat or tares? Every creature.

Jesus revealed that the enemy that sowed the tares is the devil, the enemy. The harvest is the end of the world, or literally the end of the age. At the end of the age, this harvest will occur. And the reapers are the angels. At the end of the age, the angels will come, and the lives of all unbelievers will end.

As we saw, the devil is called "the enemy" here. He is an adversary to God. It gives him great pleasure to see a human being, created in the image and likeness of God, destroyed by his own choice.

He is not satisfied with being evil himself; he wants to corrupt other people to be like he is—separated from God and living in darkness. He is actively opposing people, even though those in the world don't know it. They don't know he is trying to defeat what God is doing. And they don't know that he is not going to succeed.

Satan as "Oppressor"

The next word Satan is referred to is found in Acts 10:38, where he is called an "oppressor." He is oppressive. Whenever he comes around, the very atmosphere is oppressive. You can sense his presence!

Acts 10:38 says, *"How God anointed Jesus of Nazareth with the Holy Ghost and with power, who went about doing good, and healing all that were oppressed of the devil, for God was with him."*

Jesus healed everyone who was oppressed. Sickness is an oppression; it is the work of the enemy. Physical infirmity is oppression. Mental illness and pressure in the mental realm are oppression. Satan is the oppressor. God doesn't oppress people.

High on God

While I was working with a certain person in the ministry, I had to bite my tongue sometimes and keep quiet, because his favorite theme was, "God is going to depress you to keep you from getting too high."

I knew God doesn't do that. That's humanistic thinking. There's no such thing as being too high on God! Fill yourself with God. You can't get too full of God, and you can't overflow too much. It's not possible. The more you overflow, the more of a blessing you are, and the more people are blessed.

Do you think God gets worried that you might get too high being a blessing? He certainly doesn't give you something to lift you up and then come along and push you back down. He's not opposed to Himself—and He does not oppress or depress people.

Satan as "Thief"

The next word that describes Satan is "thief." It's found in John 10:10, where Jesus taught, *"The thief cometh not, but for to steal, and to kill, and to destroy."* That's just the opposite of what Jesus came to earth for.

Jesus continued, *"I am come that they might have life, and that they might have it more abundantly."*

So the Word of God teaches that the devil came to steal, kill, and destroy, but Jesus came to destroy the works of the devil so we could live a more abundant life. We will see killing and destroying named in other places; here we emphasize thieving.

Since Satan is a thief, his purpose is to steal. That's why the Word of God tells you to hold fast to what you have. If no one was trying to steal what you have, you wouldn't need to hold fast to it, because it wouldn't go anywhere.

When the enemy tries to steal what you have, he does it subtly. He doesn't come up to you and say, "I'm the thief—the devil—and I'm going to steal your good health." You wouldn't give it to him.

No, he doesn't operate that way; he operates subtly. First he tries to get a little foothold and finally a stronghold in your life through your wrong thinking.

If you allow wrong thinking to take hold of your mind, sooner or later it will translate into wrong actions. And when it does, Satan has a way to steal from you.

Satan as "Corrupter"

Satan is also called a "corrupter" of minds in Second Corinthians 11:3. Paul was deeply concerned that Satan might have corrupted the pure minds of the believers in Corinth.

Satan tries to corrupt minds. His main access to you is to corrupt your mind first. If he can do that, he can do other things. But if you don't let him do that, he cannot do anything else. If you keep your mind renewed by the Word of God, being a doer of the Word yourself, he will not have access to you.

Whenever he comes and fires a dart at your mind, if you're walking in the truth and believing God's Word, you will not be affected.

For example, water doesn't penetrate ducks' feathers. It lands on their outer feathers and bounces right off, so ducks don't get wet floating in the water or walking around on land in the rain.

We don't have feathers like that to protect us. However, we can insulate ourselves by knowing the Word of God and by having a renewed mind. When you have a renewed mind and the devil fires a fiery dart at you, it will bounce off you. You don't need to accept it, receive it, take the thought, or meditate on it. You just say, "That's not God. I rebuke you, devil!"

When your mind is renewed by the Word of God, you know what is of God and what isn't. It's not hard to figure out, because you know anything the devil says to you is a lie.

If he says, "You won't overcome this time," what does it prove? It proves you will overcome, because he's telling you a lie! You can console and encourage yourself, because what he is saying to you is the opposite of the truth.

Satan as "Liar" and "Murderer"

The next title Satan is referred to is "liar." In John 8:44, Jesus was speaking to the Pharisees, who were plotting to kill Him.

Understanding their intention, and trying to help them recognize the hardness of their hearts, Jesus said in verse 44, *"Ye are of your father the devil, and the lusts of your father ye will do. He was a murderer from the beginning."*

"Murderer" is another name by which Satan is called. He has come to steal and kill. He would like to murder all of us! Some people are afraid of him all the time. However, if he is as powerful as they think, we'd all be dead.

If Satan could do anything he wanted, how long do you think we'd last? He'd like to see the whole Church dead, but the whole Church isn't dead—we're delivered! That ought to show us something. Even if we only half know it, we're surviving.

Satan will kill you if you give him a way to do it. *"He was a murderer from the beginning, and abode not in the truth,"* Jesus taught, *"because there is no truth in him."* (John 8:44).

Even if the devil quotes scripture to you, it's not truth, because he always misapplies it. It's not truth when it's misapplied. The letter of the law is death, but the Spirit gives life.

If you understand the statement "there is no truth in him," whenever Satan is saying something, you know he is lying. He can't tell the truth. He has no understanding of what truth is. He is separated from light by living in darkness. There is no truth in him!

Satan as "The Father of Lies"

Jesus concluded verse 44 by saying, *"When he speaketh a lie, he speaketh of his own: for he is a liar, and the father of it."* If Satan is the father of lies, should you be involved in lying? Should you ever tell "little white lies," as they are called? No, you should never tell a lie for any purpose.

Jesus didn't lie to anyone. If He didn't want to answer a question, He simply didn't answer. When there were times when He shouldn't answer a question, He didn't answer. But He never told a lie to anyone—and you don't need to lie to anyone, either.

Someone will argue, "But there are times you need to lie to protect someone."

No, you don't. Say nothing if you can't say something that is good or edifying. My mother taught me that. She said, "If you can't say something good about someone, don't say anything." That's true. If there is no commendation for a person, don't say anything.

If you start telling little lies about something, soon you won't be able to remember what you've said. Then you'll have to tell more lies to cover up the fact that you lied. Then you'll develop a habit or a pattern of lying. You don't want to get into that.

Satan as "The Adversary"

Again, you see deception in Satan's being a murderer and a liar. The next names that describe him primarily reflect his character. The name "Lucifer" reflected his character before he fell, but he is no longer the star of the morning, the day star, or the shining one in Heaven. That's what he was; it has nothing to do with what he is today.

Fifty-two times in the Bible, he is called "Satan," which means "adversary" or "opposer." That's the literal translation of the word. As we saw in Zechariah 3:1, when the angel of the Lord appeared on earth and Joshua, the high priest, was standing before him, Satan was standing at his right hand to resist the high priest!

He is also called "Satan" in Revelation 12. That chapter calls him such things as "the devil," "that old serpent," "the great dragon," and "Satan."

In Luke 22:31, the Lord said to Peter, *"Simon, Simon, behold, Satan hath desired to have you, that he may sift you as wheat."*

Did the devil have a special desire to sift Peter as wheat? No, he has exactly the same desire to sift you! He would like to thresh out everything good in your life, and if you give him a chance, he will!

Jesus Our Intercessor

Notice what Jesus said about Peter, because it applies to you, too. *Jesus revealed that He makes continuous intercession for you!*

He said to Peter, *"But I have prayed for thee, that thy faith fail not: and when thou art converted, strengthen thy brethren"* (v. 32). He was saying, "Don't be afraid—I've prayed for you!"

When you're between the proverbial rock and the hard place sometime, think about Who is praying for you to overcome that situation. Jesus is, and He probably has some other saints praying for you, too. "Intercession" is prayer for another person. That's what Jesus Christ is doing for us in Heaven!

Jesus prayed that Peter's faith wouldn't fail. He prays the same for you, and you can be comforted, encouraged, and assured in the time of tests and trials that even though the devil desires to sift you, he won't be able to.

Satan caused Peter some problems, but who overcame—the devil or Peter? Peter did. Even though he experienced some failures along the way, he overcame them, too. We are in the same position Peter was in—in Christ!

Satan as "The Devil"

The next name for our adversary is "the devil." It's used 35 times in scripture. In one instance, Luke 4 tells how Jesus was tempted by "the devil." You will be tempted by him, too. Revelation 12:9 also calls him "the devil."

The word "devil" is a Greek word, *diabolos*. It means "slanderer" or "defamer," someone who is contrary and speaks contrary. You can tell the truth about someone, but it can be contrary to them.

For example, a brother or a sister may have committed a crime in the past, but to tell others that fact now is not godly nor necessary.

Also, when someone has missed it, you don't need to go around telling everyone what he or she did. That's not your job. Although it's true, it defames the person. Some people lie about others. That also defames them.

Some schools—even Christian schools—use the name "devil" or similar terms for their athletic teams. These include the Diablos, Blue Devils, Red Devils, Demon Deacons, and so forth.

Mount Diablo is located in the San Francisco Bay Area. There is a lot of satanic activity around that place, because everyone is always talking about it.

Why would you want to attach devilish names to athletic teams? I certainly wouldn't. Don't name things after the devil!

My wife and I were driving in a certain western state, and every sign we saw for about 60 miles was "devil this" and "demon that."

I thought, "What's the matter with the people around here? They name everything after the devil." What do you suppose results from these actions? The works of the devil. If you magnify him in people's eyes, soon he will get a foothold—and, worse, a stronghold!

Satan as "Dragon" and "Serpent"

Satan's next name is "dragon." He's called that in Revelation 12:3–17; 16:13; 20:2. Revelation 12:9 says, *"And the great dragon was cast out, that old serpent called the Devil, and Satan."*

A "dragon" is a symbol of a corrupt being; something corrupted from the way God intended it to be. Satan is certainly totally corrupted from the purpose for which God made him—and so is anyone who is like him.

His next name is "serpent," or "that old serpent," as seen in Revelation 12:9 and Second Corinthians 11. In the latter chapter, Paul was deeply concerned that, as the serpent had tempted Adam and Eve, believers in Corinth were being corrupted in their minds. The devil entered the Garden of Eden in the form of a serpent.

Many people keep snakes as pets, but they don't have much attraction for me. In fact, I rather dislike snakes, and that's probably the way it should be. God said back in the Garden of Eden that He would put enmity between the seed of the woman and the seed of the serpent. Snakes no longer reflect what God made them to be. And as we shall see, there are other members of the animal kingdom in the same situation.

Satan as "Belial"

The next name for Satan is "Belial," as seen in Second Corinthians 6:14–15: *"Be yet not unequally yoked together with unbelievers: for what fellowship hath righteousness with unrighteousness?"* The answer is: none. *"And what communion hath light with darkness?"* None. *"And what concord* [or agreement] *hath Christ with Belial?"* None.

Is there any agreement between the devil and Jesus? Of course not.

Paul continues in verses 15–18:

2 CORINTHIANS 15–18
15 ...or what part hath he that believeth with an infidel?
16 And what agreement hath the temple of God with idols?
17 Wherefore come out from among them, and be ye separate, saith the Lord, and touch not the unclean thing; and I will receive you,
18 And will be a Father unto you, and ye shall be my sons and daughters.

The name Belial indicates there is no agreement. It's also translated "wicked one" in Matthew chapter 13. The wicked one is Belial, so the name can be translated that way, too. Again, it's the opposite of what God is. Satan is entirely the opposite of God. There is no goodness in him, only wickedness.

Satan as "The Evil One"

Another name Satan is called in several scriptures is "the evil one." It's translated from two Greek words, *ho poneros*—"the evil one" or "the wicked one."

In John 17:15, Jesus prayed for His disciples (including us), *"I pray not that thou shouldest take them out of the world, but that thou shouldest keep them from the evil."*

Newer translations say *"from the evil one."* Has God done that? Yes, He has built a hedge about you. The Word of God is your defense. He has delivered you from all the power and the authority of darkness by translating you into the kingdom of His dear Son.

You have the whole armor of God and the Word of God around you to protect and keep you. When Satan was approaching God concerning touching Job, he said, "I can't touch Job. You've built a hedge around him." You have a better hedge than Job had, founded on better promises.

God Fights for You

In the Old Testament, God didn't tell His people to do much about the devil, because they weren't capable of it, and they didn't understand much about it. God did tell them to obey Him, and when they did that, He took care of the enemy for them.

When you obey God and walk in the light of God's Word, He comes on the scene and fights for you. He is a man of war, the Bible says. He does what needs to be done for you. You can't do it yourself, but when you take your dominion in the earth and speak your faith over situations, God comes on the scene and fights for you.

Can you picture yourself dealing with the devil and saying, "It is written, Jesus is my Lord!" And Jesus, your Big Brother, is standing beside you, saying, "You heard him, devil—bow your knee!" It's true. That's the way it works.

God watches over His Word to perform it. He sees to it that it comes to pass. That's *His* responsibility. *Your* responsibility is to believe that it will come to pass.

In teaching faith, we may give people the impression that confession or something like that is what makes things happen. Yes, faith has to be present for things to happen; however, it is God who performs the miracles. It is God who keeps His Word. He sees to it that what He said comes to pass.

Although you should be in faith, and your confession should be an important part of that faith, don't get the idea that *you're* making things happen. That's what God does.

God doesn't need you to tell Him *how* to do anything. All He needs from you is to believe that He will do it. And because He gave you dominion in the earth, *God is waiting for you to take that dominion by your confession of faith.*

In First John 5:18, this same expression, *ho poneros,* is used again:

1 JOHN 5:18
18 We know that whosoever is born of God sinneth not [sin is no longer your lifestyle]; but he that is begotten of God keepeth himself [by walking in the truth], and that wicked one toucheth him not.

Satan will form weapons to use against you, but they will not prosper. Although he will shoot them at you, they will be deflected, like water off a duck's back.

In Romans chapter 1, we find a perfect definition of what this Greek word, *ho poneros*, is. At the end of the chapter, it refers to all the people who are totally reprobate, have backslid, and hate God. They're like the devil, contrary to God.

ROMANS 1:31-32
31 Without understanding, covenant breakers, without natural affection, implacable, unmerciful:
32 Who knowing the judgment of God, that they which commit such things are worthy of death, not only do the same, but have pleasure in them that do them.

Reprobates take pleasure in destroying other people's lives. That's
what the devil is like. He takes pleasure in destroying lives.

Proverbs 6:26 says, *"the adulteress will hunt for the precious life."*
She wants to destroy a precious life, because she's like the devil.

The devil also wants to seek out the precious life. He's against
everyone. He's not content with being evil himself; he actively seeks
to corrupt others to become like him. Does that tell you anything about
his character?

Satan as "Destroyer"

Another name that describes his character—"destroyer"—is found
in Revelation 9:11. Previously, we saw the Greek word *Apollyon* and
the Hebrew word *Abaddon* both indicate that Satan is "a destroyer."
That's his purpose—to destroy. Apollyon/Abaddon is the king of the
bottomless pit.

Actually, some things *need* to be rooted out, pulled down, and
destroyed so something good can replace them. God has already
rooted out, pulled down, and destroyed everything in your life that
wasn't good in your spirit man.

Now you're in the process of having your mind renewed. Your
mind has been mistaken about some things, and those things need to
be rooted out and pulled down. That's all good. That's not the work of
the devil; it's the work of God.

God doesn't destroy for the sake of destroying. If He tears something down, it is so He can replace it with something better. The devil,
on the other hand, is out to destroy everything he comes in contact
with—good, bad, or indifferent. Destruction is his aim and goal. He
is the destroyer.

Satan as "Beelzebub"

We have already seen references to the last name that describes
Satan: "Beelzebub." Matthew 10:24–26 says:

MATTHEW 10:24–26

24 The disciple is not above his master, nor the servant above his lord.

25 It is enough for the disciple that he be as his master, and the servant as his lord. If they have called the master of the house [Jesus Himself] Beelzebub, how much more shall they call them of his household?

26 Fear them not therefore: for there is nothing covered, that shall not be revealed; and hid, that shall not be known.

Don't fear persecution. Don't fear people who think you are related or connected to the devil. Don't be afraid of what they think or say. It doesn't change you. If you take their words to heart, they can certainly hurt you; but if you don't believe their taunts, they won't. If someone calls me "Beelzebub," it doesn't mean that I am. It also doesn't mean that I'm going to become like that, either.

Jesus was often accused by the religious leaders of being in league with the devil. One example is found in Matthew:

MATTHEW 12:22

22 Then was brought unto him one possessed with a devil, blind and dumb: and he healed him, insomuch that the blind and dumb both spoke and saw.

That was a miracle, wasn't it? It shows Jesus going about doing good and healing those who were oppressed of the devil.

The Pharisees Accuse Jesus

The passage continues:

MATTHEW 12:23–28

23 And all the people were amazed, and said, Is not this the son of David?

24 But when the Pharisees heard it, they said, This fellow doth not cast out devils, but by *Beelzebub* the prince of the devils.

25 And Jesus knew their thoughts, and said unto them, Every kingdom divided against itself is brought to desolation; every city or house divided against itself shall not stand:

26 And if Satan cast out Satan, he is divided against himself; how shall then his kingdom stand?

27 And if I by Beelzebub [the devil, Satan] cast out devils, by whom do your children [followers, disciples] cast them out? therefore they shall be your judges.

28 But if I cast out devils by the Spirit of God, then the kingdom of God is come unto you.

Satan as "The Lord of the Flies"

Notice that Jesus called Satan *Beelzebub* here. The name "Beelzebub" literally means "lord of the flies." Why is he called "lord of the flies"? Because that represents where he has dominion and what he is truly lord over. Satan is the lord of things in darkness!

Why are flies considered to be in darkness? Because they are reprobate. Flies are so affected by the curse, they no longer do what God made them for. They don't even look like what God created them to look like.

Proof of this is seen in places where flies hang out. They get into places you don't want them to be. They don't do anything good. Flies are a pest that transmit deadly diseases.

The same holds true of mosquitoes. What good do mosquitoes do? Nothing. Mosquitoes have totally departed from the purpose for which God created them. They, too, transmit deadly diseases.

Part of the creation is reprobate like that. Satan is lord of creatures and beings that are useless, in darkness, and totally departed from what they were created for.

These are illustrations of what "Beelzebub" means. Satan is truly lord of the flies, or lord of all reprobate things that exist in darkness.

On the other hand, go out and look in a field. Even though it is somewhat under the curse, the cow you see standing there is pretty much doing what God created it to do. Cows still give milk and become food for human beings.

Satan as "The King of Terrors"

The final name describing Satan, capping all his other deceptions, is "king of terrors," found in Job 18:10–14.

JOB 18:10–14

10 The snare is laid for him in the ground, and a trap for him in the way.
11 Terrors shall make him afraid on every side, and shall drive him to his feet.
12 His strength shall be hungerbitten, and destruction shall be ready at his side.
13 It shall devour the strength of his skin: even the firstborn of death shall devour his strength.
14 His confidence shall be rooted out of his tabernacle, and it shall bring him to the *king of terrors*.

"King of terrors" describes what Satan's deceptions result in for all who follow him.

I find great comfort in remembering that James recorded in James 4:7, *"Submit yourselves therefore to God. Resist the devil, and he will flee from you."* In some translations, the phrase "flee from you" is rendered, "run from you in terror."

Yes, light *always* drives out darkness. Let *your* light shine!

Afterword

The Word of God instructs us about our authority in Christ—authority that was given to us to use in our daily walk of faith.

The same Word instructs us about Satan's devices, all of which employ lies and deception. Because we are enlightened and are no longer ignorant about these devices, the Lord says to us as He did to the apostle Paul, *"My grace is sufficient for thee: for my strength is made perfect in weakness"* (2 Cor. 12:9).

Therefore, *"Thanks be unto God, which always causeth us to triumph in Christ"* (2 Cor. 2:14).

God has set before us an *open door* which *no one* can shut (Rev. 3:8). No amount of opposition can change that fact.

So we can go forward with God. We can be and do what He has ordained for us. Remember, He called us because He knew us from the foundation of the world. He has foreordained us to be abundantly fruitful in this hour!

Always on.

For the latest news and information on products, media, podcasts, study resources, and special offers, visit us online 24 hours a day.

Free Subscription!

Call now to receive a free subscription to *The Word of Faith* magazine from Kenneth Hagin Ministries. Receive encouragement and spiritual refreshment from . . .

- *Faith-building articles from Kenneth W. Hagin, Lynette Hagin, Craig W. Hagin, Denise Hagin Burns, and others*
- *"Timeless Teaching" from the archives of Kenneth E. Hagin*
- *Feature articles on prayer and healing*
- *Testimonies of salvation, healing, and deliverance*
- *Children's activity page*
- *Updates on Rhema Bible Training College, Rhema Bible Church, and other outreaches of Kenneth Hagin Ministries*

Subscribe today for your free *Word of Faith*!

1-888-28-FAITH (1-888-283-2484)

rhema.org/wof